GREEK TRAGEDY
IN NEW TRANSLATIONS

GENERAL EDITORS
Peter Burian and Alan Shapiro

EURIPIDES: Trojan Women

EURIPIDES
Trojan Women

Translated by
ALAN SHAPIRO

with Introduction and Notes by
PETER BURIAN

OXFORD
UNIVERSITY PRESS

2009

OXFORD
UNIVERSITY PRESS

Oxford University Press, Inc., publishes works that further
Oxford University's objective of excellence
in research, scholarship, and education.

Oxford New York
Auckland Cape Town Dar es Salaam Hong Kong Karachi
Kuala Lumpur Madrid Melbourne Mexico City Nairobi
New Delhi Shanghai Taipei Toronto

With offices in
Argentina Austria Brazil Chile Czech Republic France Greece
Guatemala Hungary Italy Japan Poland Portugal Singapore
South Korea Switzerland Thailand Turkey Ukraine Vietnam

Copyright © 2009 by Oxford University Press, Inc.

Published by Oxford University Press, Inc.
198 Madison Avenue, New York, NY 10016

www.oup.com

Oxford is a registered trademark of Oxford University Press

All rights reserved. No part of this publication may be reproduced,
stored in a retrieval system, or transmitted, in any form or by any means,
electronic, mechanical, photocopying, recording, or otherwise,
without the prior permission of Oxford University Press.

Library of Congress Cataloging-in-Publication Data
Euripides.
[Trojan women. English]
Trojan women / Euripides ; translated by Alan Shapiro ; with introduction and notes by
Peter Burian.
    p. cm.
Includes bibliographical references.
ISBN 978-0-19-537493-3; 978-0-19-517910-1 (pbk.)
1. Hecuba (Legendary character)—Drama.   2. Queens—Troy
(Extinct city)—Drama.   3. Trojan War—Drama.
I. Shapiro, Alan, 1952–   II. Burian, Peter, 1943–   III. Title.
PA3975.T8S53 2008
882'.01—dc22   2008017274

EDITORS' FOREWORD

"*The Greek Tragedy in New Translations* is based on the conviction that poets like Aeschylus, Sophocles, and Euripides can only be properly rendered by translators who are themselves poets. Scholars may, it is true, produce useful and perceptive versions. But our most urgent present need is for a *re-creation* of these plays—as though they had been written, freshly and greatly, by masters fully at home in the English of our own times."

With these words, the late William Arrowsmith announced the purpose of this series, and we intend to honor that purpose. As was true of most of the volumes that began to appear in the 1970s—first under Arrowsmith's editorship, later in association with Herbert Golder—those for which we bear editorial responsibility are products of close collaborations between poets and scholars. We believe (as Arrowsmith did) that the skills of both are required for the difficult and delicate task of transplanting these magnificent specimens of another culture into the soil of our own place and time, to do justice both to their deep differences from our patterns of thought and expression and to their palpable closeness to our most intimate concerns. Above all, we are eager to offer contemporary readers dramatic poems that convey as vividly and directly as possible the splendor of language, the complexity of image and idea, and the intensity of emotion and originals. This entails, among much else, the recognition that the tragedies were meant for performance—as scripts for actors—to be sung and danced as well as spoken. It demands writing of inventiveness, clarity, musicality, and dramatic power. By such standards, we ask that these translations be judged.

This series is also distinguished by its recognition of the need of nonspecialist readers for a critical introduction informed by the best recent scholarship, but written clearly and without condescension. Each play is followed by notes designed not only to elucidate obscure references but also to mediate the conventions of the Athenian stage as well as those features of the Greek text that might otherwise go unnoticed. The notes are supplemented by a glossary of mythical and geographical terms that should make it possible to read the play without turning elsewhere for basic information. Stage directions are sufficiently ample to aid readers in imagining the action as they read. Our fondest hope, of course, is that these versions will be staged not only in the minds of their readers but also in the theaters to which, after so many centuries, they still belong.

A NOTE ON THE SERIES FORMAT

A series such as this requires a consistent format. Different translators, with individual voices and approaches to the material at hand, cannot be expected to develop a single coherent style for each of the three tragedians, much less make clear to modern readers that, despite the differences among the tragedians themselves, the plays share many conventions and a generic, or period, style. But they can at least share a common format and provide similar forms of guidance to the reader.

1. *Spelling of Greek Names*
Orthography is one area of difference among the translations that requires a brief explanation. Historically, it has been common practice to use Latinized forms of Greek names when bringing them into English. Thus, for example, Oedipus (not Oidipous) and Clytemnestra (not Klutaimestra) are customary in English. Recently, however, many translators have moved toward more precise transliteration, which has the advantage of presenting the names as both Greek and new, instead of Roman and neoclassical importations into English. In the case of so familiar a name as Oedipus, however, transliteration risks the appearance of pedantry or affectation. And in any case, perfect consistency cannot be expected in such matters. Readers will feel the same discomfort with "Athenai" as the chief city of Greece as they would with "Platon" as the author of *The Republic*.

The earlier volumes in this series adopted as a rule a "mixed" orthography in accordance with the considerations outlined above. The most familiar names retain their Latinate forms, while the rest are transliterated; -os rather than Latin -us is adopted for the termination of masculine names, and Greek diphthongs (as in Iphigeneia for Latin Iphigenia) are retained. Some of the later volumes continue this practice, but where translators have preferred to use a more consistent practice of transliteration of Latinization, we have honored their wishes.

2. *Stage Directions*

The ancient manuscripts of the Greek plays do not supply stage directions (though the ancient commentators often provide information relevant to staging, delivery, "blocking," etc.). Hence stage directions must be inferred from words and situations and our knowledge of Greek theatrical conventions. At best this is a ticklish and uncertain procedure. But it is surely preferable that good stage directions should be provided by the translator than that readers should be left to their own devices in visualizing action, gesture, and spectacle. Ancient tragedy was austere and "distanced" by means of masks, which means that the reader must not expect the detailed intimacy ("He shrugs and turns wearily away," "She speaks with deliberate slowness, as though to emphasize the point," etc.) that characterizes stage directions in modern naturalistic drama.

3. *Numbering of Lines*

For the convenience of the reader who may wish to check the translation against the original, or vice versa, the lines have been numbered according to both the Greek and English texts. The lines of the translation have been numbered in multiples of ten, and these numbers have been set in the right-hand margin. The (inclusive) Greek numeration will be found bracketed at the top of the page. The Notes that follow the text have been keyed to both numerations, the line numbers of the translation in **bold**, followed by the Greek lines in regular type, and the same convention is used for all references to specific passages (of the translated plays only) in both the Notes and the Introduction.

Readers will doubtless note that in many plays the English lines outnumber the Greek, but they should not therefore conclude that the translator has been unduly prolix. In most cases the reason is simply that the translator has adopted the free-flowing norms of modern Anglo-American prosody, with its brief-breath-and-emphasis-determined lines, and its habit of indicating cadence and caesuras by line length and setting rather than by conventional punctuation. Even where translators have preferred to cast dialogue in more regular five-beat or six-beat lines, the greater compactness of Greek diction is likely to result in a substantial disparity in Greek and English numerations.

ABOUT THE TRANSLATIONS

The translations in this series were written over a period of roughly forty years. No attempt has been made to update references to the scholarly literature in the Introductions and Notes, but each volume offers a brief For Further Reading list that will provide some initial orientation to contemporary critical thinking about the tragedies it contains.

CONTENTS

TROJAN WOMEN

INTRODUCTION

Tragedy, as everyone knows, tells "sad stories of the death of kings," but among surviving Greek tragedies only Euripides' *Trojan Women* shows us the extinction of a whole city, an entire people. Despite its grim theme, or more likely because of the way that theme resonates with the deepest fears of our own age, this is one of the relatively few Greek tragedies that regularly finds its way to the stage. The power of Euripides' theatrical and moral imagination speaks clearly across the twenty-five centuries that separate our world from his. The theme is really a double one: the suffering of the victims of war, exemplified by the women who survive the fall of Troy, and the degradation of the victors, shown by the Greeks' reckless and ultimately self-destructive behavior. *Trojan Women* gains special relevance, of course, in times of war. Today, we seem to need this play more than ever.

Let us begin, however, by considering this extraordinary document of human suffering and resilience in the context of its own times. We know that Euripides competed at the City Dionysia of 415 with a trilogy of Trojan tragedies and won second prize—almost tantamount to losing, because only three playwrights competed in the tragic competition. This information comes down to us in a bemused comment from Aelian, a writer of the early third century of our own era:

> Xenocles, whoever he was, won first prize with *Oedipus, Lykaon, Bac-chae*, and the satyr play *Athamas*; Euripides came second with *Alexan-der, Palamedes, Trojan Women*, and the satyr play *Sisyphus*. Is it not ridiculous that Xenocles should win and Euripides be defeated with plays such as these? (*Varia Historia* 2.8)

From Aelian's astonishment, we learn that in his day, Euripides' play was held in high regard, although it was not an immediate success. Aelian suggests that the only possible explanations for Euripides' loss to Xenocles were that those who voted were stupid and ignorant, or that they were bribed. Neither alternative, he says, is worthy of Athens. There are of course other possibilities. One is that Xenocles was a great writer whose works we should be very sad to have lost, but no ancient source supports this supposition. Another, perhaps more plausible, is that something about Euripides' plays offended his audience; the German philologist Wilamowitz proposed long ago that Euripides could hardly have expected to win with a tragedy such as *Trojan Women* that went so much against the grain of popular opinion.[1] That of course is also pure speculation, but there is certainly reason to think that this play did engage political issues of the day and may have struck a raw nerve in some or even most of the original audience.

When Euripides' "Trojan trilogy" was first performed, Athens was a city ostensibly at peace but feverishly preparing a massive military expedition to far-off Sicily, a war of choice whose purpose, as Thucydides describes it, was to extend Athenian power to the rich cities of the Greek west and to enrich the citizens of Athens thereby.[2] Moreover, in the years of war with Sparta and her allies, and even during the uneasy truce that was currently in force, there had been atrocities enough on both sides to make the treatment of prisoners and the sacking of cities topics of almost too immediate relevance. The Peloponnesian War broke out in 431. In 427, the city of Plateia, an ally of Athens whose attempted conquest by Thebes was one of the causes of the war, was annihilated by Sparta at Thebes' behest; its defenders were executed, its women made slaves, and the city itself razed to the ground.[3] In the same year, Athens put down revolts in several cities of Lesbos, a subject ally, and the Athenian Assembly voted to execute all males of military age in the city of Mytilene and to enslave its women and children. A ship was sent off to Mytilene to convey the decision, but on the following day, the Assembly reversed itself. Thucydides has a full account of the debate and then gives this gripping description of the dispatch of a second ship to countermand the earlier order:

> They immediately sent off another ship in great haste, lest they find the city destroyed because the first had already arrived; it was about a day and a night ahead. With the Mytilenean envoys providing wine and

---

1. U. von Wilamowitz-Moellendorff, *Griechische Tragödien Übersetzt* vol. 3(Berlin, 1906), 259.
2. As Thucydides (*History of the Peloponnesian War* 6.24) describes the popular mood prior to the expedition, passion for it

> afflicted everyone alike, the older men satisfied that either they would get control of the places they were sailing against or a great force could meet with no harm, others with the longing of youth for faraway sights and experiences and as confident of surviving as the masses were of earning money in the military for now and acquiring dominion that would provide unending service for pay.

This and all subsequent passages from Thucydides are cited in the translation of Steven Lattimore (Indianapolis and Cambridge, Mass., 1998).
3. Thucydides 3.68.

barley for the ship and making great promises if they arrived in time, the degree of zeal was so high during the voyage that they ate barley kneaded with wine and oil as they rowed, and while some rowed others slept in turns, and since by luck there was no opposing wind, and the first ship was sailing without urgency for its horrible business while this one was pressing on as described, the one ship arrived just far enough ahead that Paches had read the decree and was about to carry out what had been decided, and the ship following it landed and prevented the killings. Mytilene's danger came this close.[4]

Then, in the summer of 421, Athens besieged and recaptured Scione, an erstwhile ally in northern Greece that had revolted. In Thucydides' laconic account, the Athenians "killed the adult males, enslaving the children and women and giving the land to the Plataeans to occupy."[5] The Spartans, for their part, captured the town of Hysiae in the Argolid in the winter of 417, "killing all the free men they caught."[6]

One event, however, has long been associated with *Trojan Women*, in part because of its proximity in time to the performance of the play, and in part because one of the most famous passages in Thucydides' *History* has made it unforgettable. This is the Athenian expedition against Melos, a small island in the southern Aegean with ancestral ties to Sparta. Even after the other islands had accepted Athenian hegemony, Melos had attempted to maintain its independence. After initial Athenian raids had failed to make the Melians submit and only made them openly hostile, the Athenians sent a substantial force against the island. Thucydides gives us an extraordinary imagined dialogue preceding the hostilities in which the Melians claim that they have a right to independence and neutrality; the Athenians offer in reply, without hesitation or shame, the doctrine that might makes right. Because the power to subdue Melos is theirs, they will only appear weak if they fail to exercise it.[7]

When the Melians failed to heed their warnings, the Athenians attacked. The initial siege did not yield the desired result, so the Athenians sent reinforcements, and the Melians,

after a certain amount of treachery in their midst, surrendered to the Athenians to be dealt with as they wished. They killed all the grown men they captured, enslaved the children and women, and settled the place themselves by sending out five hundred colonists later.[8]

In the last twenty years, a number of scholars have accepted the view that there could not have been sufficient time between the destruction of

4. Thucydides 3.49.
5. Thucydides 5.32.
6. Thucydides 5.83.
7. The "Melian Dialogue," Thucydides 5.85–113.
8. Thucydides 5.116.

Melos—probably no earlier than December 416—and the production of *Trojan Women* in March 415 for the play to have been written in response to the Melian disaster.[9] How quickly Euripides might have responded to events (and the Melian siege, after all, went on for a considerable time, with its outcome not hard to imagine), and how those events might have shaped or reshaped part of his trilogy, is obviously difficult to say. But even if Melos was not on Euripides' mind when he wrote the play, it is even more difficult to suppose that the practices of warfare it portrays from the vantage point of the victim could have nothing to do with war and politics in his own day. That these practices were still a regular feature of Greek warfare we have just seen; that they were a subject of intense and passionate argument in Athens in the years preceding Melos is made clear by Thucydides' report about the debate in the Assembly that led to the rescinding of the "death order" for Mytilene.[10] And because, as N. T. Croally sensibly points out, the performance took place some months after the fall of Melos, the writing of the play is not necessarily the most important moment to consider; rather, "it was a matter for the audience to decide in March whether they saw the play as a response (as *their* response) to Melos."[11]

In reading *Trojan Women* with knowledge of the extreme destructiveness with which resistance was likely to be met at the time, cognizance of Athens' imperial ambitions (especially with the impending Sicilian expedition in the air) and Sparta's fears on that account, and

9. Proposed by A. van Erp Taalman Kip, "Euripides and Melos," *Mnemosyne* 40 (1987): 414–9. It should be said that this decoupling of Melos from *Trojan Women* has been welcomed as a way to defang the play politically. D. Kovacs, "Gods and Men in Euripides' Trojan Trilogy," *Colby Quarterly* 33 (1997): 162–76, uses this argument as the basis for rejecting interpretations of *Trojan Women* as a document with specific relevance to Athenian policy or politics altogether. Instead, he suggests, the play should be understood in the Greek poetic tradition that emphasized the instability of fortune and the fallibility of human understanding. Kovacs underlines the "paradoxical consolation" that the great misfortunes shown, remembered, and predicted in the play are not the product of accident or mere human folly, but of divine will. *Trojan Women*, then, is a philosophical and religious document, but hardly a political one. J. Roisman, "Contemporary Allusions in Euripides' *Trojan Women*," *Studi italiani di filologia classica*, 3rd ser., 15 (1997): 38–46, also rules Melos out of consideration but is nevertheless open to the notion that the play makes "conscious references to contemporary events and opinions," even if they should not "be construed as its dominant element." It turns out, however, that the only allusions he approves of are those that do not suggest criticism of Athenian imperial policy. Thus, for example, Roisman acknowledges the possibility of a contemporary reference in Cassandra's commendation of the Trojans for fighting a war that was forced upon them and waged in and for their homeland, and in her condemnation of the Greeks for fighting by choice, far from home. He does not think, however, that this would raise questions about the impending invasion of Sicily, since in his view few Athenians at the time "would have regarded the Sicilian expedition as a moral dilemma." Although he does allow the possibility of multiple meanings for different audiences, he argues that Euripides' "conscious references" provide "the option of rejecting a recognition of themselves in the depiction of the Greeks." That was an option, then as now, but not the only one by any means.

10. The "Mytilenean Debate," Thucydides 3.35–50.

11. N. T. Croally, *Euripidean Polemic: The Trojan Women and the Function of Tragedy* (Cambridge, 1994), 232, n. 170.

familiarity with the exasperated rhetoric of power that this and other Euripidean tragedies share with Thucydides, encourages us to understand it as a specifically political, singularly dark, and deeply humane drama. If a reading of *Trojan Women* that depends on its direct inspiration by a particular historical event is open to the charge of anachronism, an interpretation that treats it as a demonstration (quoting Kovacs) "that uncertainty about the future is the human condition's most salient feature, and that it is the part of a wise man not to take today's happiness for granted"[12] is open to the charge of being reductive and historically impoverished. But there is no reason to suppose that we must choose one reading or the other. *Trojan Women* presents a particularly intense account of human suffering and uncertainty, but one that is also rooted in considerations of power and policy, morality and expedience. Furthermore, the seductions of power and the dangers both of its exercise and of resistance to it as portrayed in *Trojan Women* are not simply philosophical or rhetorical gambits; they are part of the lived experience of Euripides' day, in Greek and Athenian action and argument. Their analogues in our own day lie all too close at hand.

EURIPIDES' "TROJAN TRILOGY"

The passage from Aelian quoted above provides valuable information that is often missing with regard to other tragedies: the names of the plays that preceded *Trojan Women* (*Alexander* and *Palamedes*) and of the satyr play (*Sisyphus*) that completed the tetralogy mandated by the rules of the City Dionysia. While the subject of *Sisyphus* can only be guessed at,[13] enough remains by way of fragments and other testimonia to make possible a rough reconstruction of the first two plays, which together with *Trojan Women* clearly constituted an interconnected set of Trojan tragedies, if not precisely a tight trilogic structure like that of Aeschylus's

---

12. Kovacs (above, n. 9), 176.

13. Only two short fragments of the satyr play survive, not enough to permit even the identification of its mythical plot. One of them, however, is addressed to Heracles, and the only myth known to connect Sisyphus and Heracles is the story of the horses of Diomedes that Heracles brought to Eurystheus as one of his famous labors. These horses were then stolen by Sisyphus, who gave them to his son Glaucus, whom they then devoured. A satyr play could be made from some part of this story, but there are other possibilities in which Heracles might play a role. One with greater relevance to the Trojan tragedies is the tale of Sisyphus seducing Anticleia and becoming the real father of Odysseus. Discussion of *Sisyphus* is complicated by the existence of a well-known and remarkable fragment of forty-two lines that has every earmark of coming from a satyr play. The fragment gives a narrative of the rise of human culture that culminates with a wise man inventing the gods to instill fear in evildoers and keep human behavior within the bounds of law. Our main source for this fragment, the skeptical philosopher Sextus Empiricus, attributes it to Critias, an aristocratic Athenian contemporary of Euripides, who wrote poems and dramas and became a leader of the Thirty Tyrants at the end of the Peloponnesian War. Two other writers, however, quote parts of the fragment and attribute them to Euripides; one of them, Aetius, says Sisyphus is the speaker, a view shared by some modern scholars. The style of the passage makes Euripidean authorship problematic, but not impossible.

Oresteia.[14] As far as we can determine, this is the only time when Euripides presented three tragedies that present successive phases of the same legendary subject: all three plays take place at or near Troy and treat Trojan War themes in chronological order. In the case of *Alexander*, a papyrus from the Egyptian town of Oxyrhynchus from the second century of our era gives us a fragmentary plot summary of the play. There are also a couple of papyrus fragments from the play itself, as well as a number of "book fragments," the majority of which are quotations preserved by the later anthologist John of Stobi (or Stobaeus). In addition, we have several fragments of an *Alexander* by the early Roman poet Ennius, including chunks from Cassandra's prophecy of the downfall of Troy, that are almost surely related to the Euripidean play.

Using these materials, a reconstruction of *Alexander* is possible: Alexander is a son of King Priam and Queen Hecuba, exposed on a mountainside and given up for dead because his mother dreamt that she had given birth to a burning torch, which Apollo's oracle interpreted to mean that this son, if he grew up, would be the destruction of Troy. Alexander was rescued by a herdsman and given the name Paris, the name by which we have come to know him. All this was presumably recounted, perhaps by Aphrodite, in the prologue. Twenty years later, Paris is brought to Troy by fellow herdsmen and arraigned before Priam because of the arrogant way he treats them—an indication, as it later turns out, that he is not one of them. He defends himself and is even allowed to take part in commemorative games that Hecuba, mourning the loss of her son, had established in Alexander's honor, though he must first overcome the opposition of his brother Deiphobus, who thinks him a slave and thus ineligible to compete. Stobaeus preserves parts of what seems to be a debate between Deiphobus and Paris. Paris's victory in the footrace and pentathlon (reported by a messenger) further enrages Deiphobus, who returns from the games berating Hector for taking his defeat at the hands of a slave too lightly. Deiphobus plots with Hecuba to kill the upstart (the papyrus preserves a bit of this), although Cassandra, in a frenzied state, recognizes him for who he is and prophesies the destruction of Troy. She is of course given no credence. Two lines preserved by Stobaeus show that Paris learns of the danger to his life. The herdsman who raised Paris is compelled by this danger to tell the truth about his supposed child's origin, and Hecuba is prevented from killing Paris, presumably at the last moment. She has found the lost son she had mourned for so long, and paradoxically, in failing to kill him now, she destroys her city. Present joy plays out against the foreboding of disaster to come.

---

14. Text and translation of the fragments, along with judicious commentary and further bibliography, are available in C. Collard, M. J. Cropp, and G. Gibert, eds., *Euripides: Selected Fragmentary Plays*, vol. 2 (Oxford, 2004).

Considerably less material survives from *Palamedes*, and reconstruction depends largely on versions found in the mythographers and other late sources. Because we are aware of additional dramas on this theme by Aeschylus, Sophocles, and Astydamas the Younger, a fourth-century tragedian, it is hard to be sure which of the variants in our surviving sources should be attributed to Euripides' play.[15] All versions, however, have enough in common to allow us to give an outline of the plot with some confidence. Palamedes is a man known for his intelligence (in one of the surviving fragments, he claims to be the inventor of writing, a skill that will play a crucial role in the plot), and for this and other reasons he wins the jealousy and enmity of Odysseus and other Greek commanders, including Agamemnon, whom Palamedes may have personally insulted.[16] Odysseus devises a deadly plot against Palamedes: he buries gold under Palamedes' tent and forges a letter, purportedly from Priam, promising that amount of gold for Palamedes' betrayal of the Greeks. The play features a trial scene pitting Odysseus's clever sophistry against Palamedes' wisdom, presumably with Agamemnon as judge. Palamedes is sentenced to be stoned to death. In a device of Palamedan ingenuity, his brother Oeax chisels a message on oar blades and launches them into the sea, hoping that one will reach their father Nauplius (the "fragment" we have in which he does this is actually a parody of the Euripidean lines from Aristophanes' *Thesmophoriazusae* of 411). The message does reach Nauplius, and he apparently arrives at the end of the play to threaten revenge.

Clearly, aspects of these plays bear upon *Trojan Women*. Euripides gives us one drama that explores the origins of the war, another connected with the Greek siege of Troy, and (in *Trojan Women*) a third that presents the devastating consequences of Troy's fall.[17] At least two characters from *Alexander*, Hecuba and Cassandra, reappear in *Trojan Women*. Assuming that the surviving fragments of Ennius' *Alexander* follow the Euripidean original closely, the disastrous events foretold in Cassandra's prophecy all come to pass in *Trojan Women*. The image of fire of which Hecuba dreams at the beginning of *Alexander* returns to engulf her city at the end of *Trojan Women*. The Odysseus whom Hecuba rages so vehemently against in *Trojan Women* has shown himself to be a villainous liar in

---

15. R. Scodel, *The Trojan Trilogy of Euripides*, Hypomnemata 60 (Göttingen, 1980), makes the most thorough attempt to reconstruct and evaluate the lost plays of the trilogy (although she perhaps overemphasizes the connections between them and *Trojan Women*), and she does what one can to sort out the specifically Euripidean elements in the Palamedes tradition; see pp. 43–63. Since Scodel wrote, however, there is new evidence to suggest that Nauplius, Palamedes' father, appeared at the end of the play to threaten revenge for his son's death; see Collard et al., 92–5.

16. See Plato *Republic* 522d.

17. See F. Dunn, *Tragedy's End: Closure and Innovation in Euripidean Drama* (New York and Oxford, 1996), 112–3. Dunn points out that no other dramatic trilogy or single epic poem encompasses the beginning, middle, and end of the Troy story.

Palamedes, and the ruin of the Greeks promised by Nauplius at the end of that play is taken up by the gods in the prologue of the next.

Given that this grouping of such closely connected plays is unique in Euripides, one would very much like to know what the connections signify. Answers to this question have varied greatly, and what remains of the plays makes it hard to say anything definitive. It seems unlikely, however, that the lost plays contained a comforting answer to the suffering of the defeated Trojan women in our play. It is certain that *Alexander* shows the beginnings of a sequence of events that *Trojan Women* will complete, but only in the sense that *Alexander* set something in motion that cannot be called back. The events of this play do not explain or justify the results that will somehow issue from them, nor are they said to do so in *Trojan Women*. Palamedes contrasts the ways in which human ingenuity can be used to creative and destructive ends and shows how the self-serving side of our nature can push us to abandon all decency. This observation offers one explanation for the Greeks' destruction after their triumph at Troy, but the gods who promise that destruction at the beginning of *Trojan Women* ignore that explanation and offer their own instead. The linkage of themes is real but far from simple, and the wish to see some justice and order emerge from all the horror of Troy will not be satisfied.

WHAT'S HECUBA TO US?

Although *Trojan Women* continues to be performed regularly and to make its impact felt on audiences worldwide, until quite recently its critical reputation did not match its success on stage. Scholars steeped in the tradition of Aristotle's *Poetics* criticized a tragedy that had the temerity to offer no reversal of fortune, but simply sufferings piled one upon the other to the breaking point. For much of the nineteenth and twentieth centuries, the view of the famous German critic A. W. Schlegel carried great weight. He found the "accumulation of helpless suffering" wearisome to the point of exhaustion, objected to Hecuba as a protagonist who could only lament, and characterized the debate between Helen and Hecuba as a sterile rhetorical exercise.[18] Such objections were repeated for more than a century in harsh and condescending terms: "static," "almost plotless," padded with "dry and analytic rhetoric." Even the distinguished translator Richmond Lattimore expressed a sort of grudging bemusement: "In candor, one can hardly call *The Trojan Women* a good piece of work, but it seems nevertheless to be a great tragedy."[19]

Theatrical producers and audiences have accepted its greatness more open-handedly. Particularly in the twentieth century, there seems to have

18. A. W. Schlegel, *A Course of Lectures on Dramatic Art and Literature*, trans. John Black (London, 1846), 136–7.
19. "Introduction" to *Trojan Women*, in D. Grene and R. Lattimore, eds., *Euripides III* (Chicago, 1958), 135.

been a strong sense that this drama speaks to the horrors of war in our time as well as its own. From Franz Werfel's adaptation, *Die Troerinnen*, written and produced in the midst of World War I, and Gilbert Murray's translation, which successfully toured the United States, sponsored by the Women's Peace Party as war clouds gathered on these shores in 1915, to Jean-Paul Sartre's adaptation, *Les Troyennes*, written in response to the French war in Algeria, the striking film version made by Michael Cacoyannis during the Vietnam War (following a stage run of more than 650 performances in New York), Tadashi Suzuki's adaptation, also from the 1970s, in which the play is set in Japan after the Second World War, and many others more recently, *Trojan Women* has asserted its claim as the most grippingly contemporary of Greek tragedies.[20]

Clearly, watching this play—at least with the mind's eye—helps one understand what makes it so powerful, despite its apparent flaws. It is almost a cliché to say that Greek tragedies are drama of words, not deeds. Actors stand around and argue, choruses rehearse the mythic background, prayers and laments resound. The murders, the battles, the blindings all take place off stage, and the audience finds out about them from the speeches of messengers. Yet there is every reason to be skeptical of Aristotle's claim in the *Poetics* that tragedy can be fully experienced through reading alone.[21] In what follows, we will examine how attention to movement and gesture, and even to the externals of "spectacle" (*opsis* in Aristotelian terminology),[22] can inflect and deepen our understanding of the words; and I shall also point out some ways in which performance elements are themselves enhanced by particular features of the verbal texture, particularly in its characteristic alternation of speech and song. Our evidence for the Greek tragedy is largely in the form of scripts to which modern editors must add even the most rudimentary stage directions. Happily, however, these scripts contain most of the information we need to make reasonable conjectures

---

20. Werfel's version was published at Leipzig in 1915. Murray's translation, also published in 1915, had been produced already in 1905, implicitly reflecting his opposition to the Boer War; see E. Hall and F. Macintosh, *Greek Tragedy and the British Theatre 1660–1914* (Oxford, 2005), 508–11. Sartre wrote his adaptation in 1964; it was first performed in a Paris production directed by Cacoyannis in 1965, appeared as a book in 1966, and in English translation by Ronald Duncan in 1967. The Cacoyannis film, with Katherine Hepburn as Hecuba, was released in 1971, its text (like that of his New York theatrical production) being an adaptation of Edith Hamilton's translation. Suzuki's *Toroia no Onna* was first staged in Tokyo in 1974, then revived for an international tour that began in 1977 and ended in 1990. There is information on several of these productions in M. McDonald, *The Living Art of Greek Tragedy* (Bloomington, 2003), 147–50.

21. *Poetics* 62a12.

22. *Poetics* 50b17–20. Aristotle calls *opsis* the "least artistic and least integral to the poetic art" of all the elements of tragedy. G. F. Else, *Aristotle's Poetics: The Argument* (Cambridge, Mass., 1957), 278–9, makes a case for the view that Aristotle refers only to costume and mask, but *opsis* has regularly been understood as the visual element of tragedy as a whole, and Aristotle's deprecation of it has led to its exclusion from much traditional criticism.

about blocking, choreography, and even gesture, although much uncertainty obviously remains in matters of detail. Whatever the obstacles, however, attention to these aspects of ancient theater will help us to follow Aristotle's advice to poets to "construct the plot and work it out in dialogue while keeping it before one's eyes as much as possible."[23]

Seen this way, for all its lack of obvious action, *Trojan Women* is not simply a *pathos*, an extended suffering; it is a *drama*, a "doing" that is both gripping and disturbing, the drama of life going on in the face of disaster and despair. The play opens with what might be described as a "silent action."[24] Although the text begins with a monologue spoken by the sea god Poseidon, his words "there is Hecuba" (43/36) imply that the old queen, robed in black, her hair shorn, has already been helped on stage by her attendants. Spectators will surely be expecting her to speak, but instead, she collapses, buries her head in her arms, and remains motionless. Only after a brief pause, then, does Poseidon enter to announce that he is abandoning the city he had protected until its fall. The picture of desolation is all the more poignant for being painted by the god who had built the walls that Athena has now succeeded in destroying (54-7/45-7). Hardly is the goddess's name out when she herself enters to engage Poseidon in a truce and common action against the Greeks, who in victory have outraged her. Thus, the prologue looks ahead, beyond the bounds of the play, to the destruction of the Greek fleet, the sufferings and deaths of the conquerors, in short to a future of continued hatred and devastation for those in whom triumph has bred sacrilegious excess. Poseidon's speech and the subsequent dialogue with Athena, the settling of scores and the promise of horror still to come, confirmed by the audience's knowledge of the tradition of the Greeks' disastrous homeward journey, are played out against the tableau of the pitiful but regal figure of Hecuba, prostrate with grief. Poseidon, who points her out "if anyone cares to see" (43/36), stresses the old queen's wretchedness. Seeing Hecuba there, motionless and mute, not only gives palpable human substance to the gods' talk of destruction and misery, but also emphasizes the contrast between their power and the helplessness of humans.

---

23. *Poetics* 55a23. For Aristotle, this seems to mean above all the proper guiding of the stage action by visualizing the whereabouts of characters both on and off stage. For us, it can imply attention to everything that is done on stage and in the orchestra, the drama in its most literal sense.

24. I use this term to describe actions, implied in numerous tragic and comic texts, that take place before the first words of the prologue are spoken; see P. Burian, "The Play Before the Prologue: Initial Tableaux on the Greek Stage," in J. H. D'Arms and J. W. Eadie, eds., *Ancient and Modern: Essays in Honor of Gerald F. Else* (Ann Arbor, 1977), 79–94. The Greek theater had no curtain, and the traditional view requires that when actors who were not going to initiate the dialogue took their places on stage in full view of the audience, their entrance was simply to be ignored, or rather "erased as though it had not happened" when the prologue got under way (O. Taplin, "Aeschylean Silences and Silence in Aeschylus," *Harvard Studies in Classical Philology* 76 [1972]: 62). There is, however, no need to treat these entrances so apologetically, and every reason to treat them as significant starting points for what follows.

The gods depart; only now does Hecuba stir and begin her lament. If this discussion of *Trojan Women* focuses in large part on Hecuba, it is because from the moment the gods leave the scene until the very end of the play, Hecuba remains at the center of the action, singing, chanting, and speaking nearly a fourth of the lines, never out of our sight. Gesture and movement play a crucial role here, reinforcing the affective power of the language. At the start of her first chant, she still lies on the ground, just raising her head; then, as the text clearly indicates, she sits up, rocking her body back and forth in a gesture of mourning. She will collapse again when Cassandra is led away to become the concubine of Agamemnon, and her first long speech is made from the ground where she has fallen. But she will rise again to receive the successive blows that rain down upon herself, her family, her ruined city. Only at the end of the play, when she is being led into captivity, does she break free at last and try to rush into burning Troy. She is stopped from this escape, and we see her fall to earth one last time to beat the ground with her fists, as if to rouse the shades of her dead, then rise one last time to lead her fellow captives into their new lives.

Returning to Hecuba's first lament, the emotional effect of the old queen's arousal from the depths of silent despair is amplified by the fact that she rouses herself to song. Her words are couched in an anapestic rhythm that allows itself to modulate from spoken or chanted verse to a fully lyric form accompanied, as Hecuba rises, by the plangent tones of the *aulos*, an ancient oboe-like double-reed instrument. There is a touching contrast between the divine prologue, spoken in the standard iambic verse of tragic dialogue, and this passionate, painfully human lament. Hecuba combines a bitter acknowledgment of loss with the grudging recognition that mourning itself provides some relief in the midst of sorrow:

> this long lament,
> These tears, the only music
> Left for the wretched, singing the song
> Of troubles no one dances to.   (137–40/119–21)

The fallen queen speaks these words just before her lament moves from chant to full song. The "troubles no one dances to" are, in the lapidary Greek, "dooms without dance" (*atas achoreutous*); what an odd thing to say in a medium defined formally by the presence of the chorus, and in a play whose chorus will indeed dance these very dooms! This curious bit of self-consciousness, the questioning of the power of representation to represent what this play is intent on representing, points to the unique extremity of the "troubles" in *Trojan Women*. As Adrian Poole remarked, this play is "Euripides' *Endgame*."[25] And yet the release, the relief of song drives Hecuba to rise and sing.

25. "Total Disaster: Euripides' *Trojan Women*," *Arion*, n.s., 3 (1976): 257.

Hecuba's "undanceable" lament prompts the entrance of the Chorus of Trojan captives. As elsewhere in Euripides, their arrival is motivated by what is said on stage; in this case, one part of the Chorus enters immediately in answer to Hecuba's request to join her in grieving, and the second part arrives in answer to the appeal of the first. The emotional involvement of these women with the action on stage is immediately established by their anxious questions about their own futures, expressed in the same anapestic rhythms Hecuba has been using. They subsume the individual suffering of the fallen queen into a collective gesture of solidarity, joining her in a ritual performance that helps all the afflicted come to terms with their grief and carry on. In the course of this lyric dialogue (*kommos*), the Chorus move from bewailing their misfortune to imagining a future as slaves of the victors—where will they go, what will their lives be like? The Trojan captives do not attempt to sing and dance the "troubles no one dances to"; indeed, this is the only choral song in the play that does not concentrate on Troy. Rather, moving as Hecuba had before from chanted to lyric anapests, they speculate about where their new masters will take them—let it be Athens, not Sparta, or at least Thessaly, or beautiful Sicily. The heightened emotion of the Chorus's entrance song, then, serves not to deepen the prologue further but rather to lighten its grimness. In the music and movement that enact human solidarity, in the consolations of ritual lament, a resurgence of life force manifests itself, ready to meet what the future holds.

This concern for the future makes an emotional about-face with the arrival of the Greek herald Talthybius, who announces the destinies of Hecuba's daughters Cassandra and Polyxena and her daughter-in-law Andromache, and finally Hecuba's own fate. The news goes from bad to worse: Cassandra, to whom Apollo gave the privilege of remaining unmarried, must serve as Agamemnon's concubine; Polyxena has been mysteriously enslaved to Achilles' tomb; Andromache will belong to Neoptolemus, the son of her husband Hector's slayer. Hecuba has been allotted to the treacherous and hateful Odysseus. This scene provides an excellent example of the effects possible in a *kommos* where one participant speaks in iambics and the other responds in highly charged outbursts of lyric. Talthybius answers Hecuba's questions with calm and tact in single iambic lines, and she responds to the news in lyric meters, reaching the highest pitch of anguish and vehement denunciation, expressed in violent rhythms, when she learns that she herself is to serve Odysseus. The contrasting use of meter and mode of delivery conveys more than differing levels of emotional engagement: Talthybius' laconic calm underlines the starkness of the reality he announces, while Hecuba's lyric intensity conveys the full force, even in utter powerlessness, of her emotional resistance.

Hecuba's response to her new sorrows, however, is not the whole story. The lines with which the Chorus Leader in Greek tragedy conventionally caps a scene here answer Hecuba's plea that the Chorus weep for her with a reminder of their own misery: "Your fate is known, my lady. But what of mine, / Who'll be my master? What Achaean, what Greek?" (324–5/292–3). It is a striking feature of *Trojan Women* that the ordinary women of Troy not only reflect and amplify the grief of the royal family but also call attention to their own. Hecuba's fate as fallen queen is, as it were, the traditional tragic subject, but Euripides keeps reminding us that she is now as much a slave as the women who were once her slaves and retainers, and that their sorrows are now very much like her own. Furthermore, Hecuba—and, as we shall see, her daughter-in-law Andromache—respond not simply as royals fallen from their former high estate, but also as ordinary women caught up in extraordinary circumstances, as wives and mothers bereft of their loved ones, expressing the sense of bereavement, the anguish, and even the hopes that are the normal human response to such extremity.

Cassandra, on the other hand, is a special case, and her entrance is a genuine *coup de théâtre*: Talthybius's call for Cassandra to be brought out for delivery to her new master is forestalled by the sight of flames from within the women's huts. He thinks that they have chosen to burn themselves alive; no, says Hecuba, that is not a blaze, it is my frenzied child Cassandra running toward us. And Cassandra rushes through the doorway, brandishing flaming torches, singing and dancing a mad parody of a wedding hymn. Fittingly, music and movement upstage iambic speech altogether. Cassandra's sudden, turbulent eruption onto the stage is a spectacular moment, but also horrible in its seeming flight from sanity. The imagined marriage in Apollo's temple is of course a mocking parody of her enslavement to the bed of Agamemnon, but it rests ironically on the expected wish-dream of a maiden for marriage, and it forms with equal irony the prelude to Cassandra's promise, in her subsequent speech, to exact vengeance from Agamemnon for the fall of Troy. Apollo's virgin votary calls on the god to lead the dance that consecrates her to marriage, and upon the Trojan women "in all your finery" (388/348) to join the celebration—irony made visible, given the miserable dress of the women we see before us.

Hecuba talks Cassandra down, as we might say, takes the torches from her hands, and has them carried away, but as in Aeschylus's *Agamemnon*, Cassandra, rather than subsiding into silence, turns to plain speech (i.e., the iambics of tragic dialogue) that explains the meaning of her wild performance with a lucidity that is anything but mad. She offers a clear-eyed, prophetic view of the role that she will play in Agamemnon's murder and the destruction of Atreus's house: her marriage will be "more disastrous than Helen's," her wedding night "a night of death /

And devastation" (410–2/357–60). Recounting the death and pain the Greeks inflicted and suffered "for just one woman's sake" (422/368), Cassandra makes a carefully constructed, if paradoxical, case that it is they who in the end will taste defeat, whereas Troy, whose warriors fought nobly in defense of their own soil, will have won undying fame. The Chorus Leader caps this speech by calling Cassandra "giddy" and her speech "dark" (470–1/406–7); we are reminded that Apollo blighted Cassandra's gift of prophecy with the curse that she would never be understood. Talthybius responds by forgiving Cassandra's words of ill omen only because she is mad, and even questioning Agamemnon's judgment in taking her as his bedmate.

Even after Talthybius instructs Cassandra to follow him to the ships, she stands fast and delivers a second prophetic message, describing in some detail the sufferings of the Greeks on their homeward voyage. Changing to more solemn trochaic verse for an address to her "bride-groom," she foretells that the man who brags of sacking Troy will be buried "dishonorably, by night" (513–5/445–7). Cassandra then enacts her withdrawal from service to Apollo with a striking gesture, bidding farewell to the woolen headbands that are tokens of her priestly office by tearing them from her brow and flinging them to the wind.[26] She ends this final, powerful speech by embracing the horror of her own death, which will seal her final victory over Troy's enemies as she goes "tri-umphant" (538/460) to join the dead below.

Hecuba, who has heard her daughter's prophecy but cannot under-stand her death as anything but another terrible loss, is overcome and collapses. The Chorus Leader urges her attendants to lift her up, but Hecuba says she will remain where she has fallen "from all I suffer and have suffered, and / For all the suffering still to come" (547–8/467–8). And yet she gathers the strength to tell her story, if only for the satisfaction of rousing fresh pity in her listeners. This iambic speech is the pendant to her lyrical lament in the prologue, and it is the only other opportunity for an extended account of her own story—the good fortune that once was hers, the horrors she has witnessed, and the future she fears—rather than a response to the sorrows of her kin. At some point in this speech clearly she rises, reanimated by passionate engagement in what she recounts. Then, at the end, after she has returned to Cassandra, Polyxena, and all the children she has lost, who can give her neither aid or comfort, she asks to be led—as she had been in the "silent action" that preceded the prologue—to a place where she can lie down "and cry myself into oblivion" (594/508–9).

---

26. See the note on 524–5 for the relation of this gesture to that of Cassandra in Aeschylus's *Agamemnon*.

After the long series of speeches that closed the first episode comes tragedy's quintessential leap from speech to song: the Chorus of Trojan women sing and dance their first episode-dividing ode or *stasimon*, taking us from the immediate world of the action to project in word, music, and mimetic movement the larger picture of the city's fall. They do not quite dance the "troubles no one dances to," however, for they frame the city's fall in a beguiling evocation of the relief and joy that first greeted news of the wooden horse, and the dances and songs that greeted its arrival—all of course made poignant in the retelling by knowledge of what was still to come. Similarly, the second stasimon will dance around Troy's destruction by describing an earlier sacking and burning of the city by Heracles and Telamon, and then considering the gods' present indifference to Troy's present fate. Only the third stasimon, which follows the departure of the hated Helen, will translate the city's destruction directly into movement, gesture, and song; and even here, the first images are nostalgic ones of rites and places now lost. This sensuous evocation serves, however, as a bitter reproach to Zeus, whom the Chorus sees as having abandoned their city. The destruction itself is evoked in startlingly personal terms, as the women address first their slaughtered husbands, wandering unburied, and then evoke the words of the children frightened at being separated from their mothers as they are led away for the journey to come.

The second episode begins with another notable arrival, one that sets a tone entirely different from that of Cassandra's spectacular entrance. Hector's widow, Andromache, enters from the wings in a cart laden with the arms of Hector and other spoils, her young son Astyanax in her arms. She is bound for the ship of her new master, Neoptolemus. As with Cassandra's torch-dance, the point is not just to create an arresting spectacle, but also to provide an appropriate visual reference point for the entire episode. Here is the loving wife of the greatest Trojan hero, about to be delivered to the son of her husband's slayer, along with their child. The cart that they share with the rest of the spoils emphasizes their status as just so much booty to be disposed of by their captors, "mere loot, nobility in the great turning / Of the wheel become the slaves of others," as she herself bitterly observes (709–10/614–5). And as with Cassandra's casting off of her priestly regalia in the preceding episode, there seems to be a pointed allusion to Aeschylus's *Oresteia*. The grand entrance of Agamemnon in his royal chariot in the *Agamemnon* is the obvious model for this scene. The outward contrast could hardly be greater; the victorious generalissimo with spoils of war in tow, including Cassandra, makes a triumphal return. And yet of course he is heading, all unknowing, to his ignominious doom. For Andromache, too, a further and unexpected reversal is in store.

The presence of Astyanax is crucial, for it is he who inspires Hecuba, pragmatic and intent on survival in the face of every new horror, with hope—and he whose fate will strike the final blow. The episode begins, unusually, with a *kommos*, a lyric duet between Andromache and Hecuba whose main formal feature is a large number of split verses, as if a regular pattern of line exchange was inadequate for the emotions of the grieving women. This gives way to a spoken exchange in which Andromache reveals that Polyxena has been sacrificed at Achilles' tomb (the explanation of Talthybius' mysterious words in the preceding episode, and the next blow the old queen must endure),[27] and argues, by way of consolation, that Polyxena's fate is better than her own: "She's better off than I am, still alive." To this Hecuba replies unhesitatingly, "No, child, you're wrong. They're not the same. / Life means hope, death is nothing at all" (727–9/630–3). After Andromache's elaborate and passionate exposition of her reasons for preferring death to the life she now faces, in which she must either accept a new lord and betray her beloved Hector, or show her hostility and face his wrath, Hecuba replies by invoking Astyanax as the future of Troy. Accept your new master, she says, and your lot, so that you can bring up my grandson. "And maybe his descendants will come home / To Troy and bring the city back to life" (809–10/703–5).

Hardly are these words out, however, when Talthybius reappears and haltingly brings himself to announce that the Greeks have decided to kill the boy—so much for the one remaining hope for Troy! Talthybius, quite surprisingly for a herald, shows shame at his fellow Greeks' actions and sympathy for the victims: "Against my will, I must announce the common / Will of the Greeks," he tells Andromache, asking her not to hate him for it (815–7/710–11). Shame and sympathy are both manifest in the hesitancy with which Talthybius makes the announcement in slow, painful stages and in the advice he gives. He urges Andromache to "grieve nobly, befitting your nobility" (835/727), reminding her that she is utterly powerless ("your city / Ruined, your husband dead," 838–9/730) and that the Greeks can easily handle "just one woman" (841/731)—a remark made more poignant by the glancing allusion to Helen, the "one woman" so often mentioned in this play, who caused so many years of grief. He advises her not to do anything that would make the army angry, lest they refuse even burial to her dead child.

For Andromache, after a powerful speech that seizes on the paradox of Greek barbarity and ends with a tremendous curse against Helen, there is nothing left to do but abandon her child to his executioners, and herself to her fate: "But go on, take him, / Carry him off, hurl him [*rhiptete*] to his destruction" (888–9/774), she commands in the bitterness of total despair, adding that they should cover her body "and hurl me [*rhiptete*] / Into

27. For this technique, see note on 666.

the ship's hold" (893–4/778). In a heart-wrenching moment of separation, Talthybius takes the child toward the city, Andromache's cart is dragged toward the shore, and it is left to Hecuba speak the lament for her grandson, just as later she will perform his burial rites. The contrast of naked force and human compassion could hardly be more explicit.

At this point it is perhaps worth stopping for a moment to observe how variegated a picture Euripides presents of the three women whose struggles and sufferings we have been following. All are caught up in a single, terrible doom, but each of them is so fully personalized and differentiated that rather than becoming numbed by the succession of sorrows, we come to feel for each woman as an individual. All of them have known wealth and privilege, and all are now in positions of seemingly absolute weakness; each is strong in her own particular way. Cassandra derives her strength from her role as virgin priest and prophet, able to turn her forced concubinage with Agamemnon into a sacral celebration because she knows that it will give her vengeance for the sacrilege done to her and the destruction wrought upon her city, her family, and her people. Andromache paradoxically suffers because of her nature as a loving and loyal wife, which is also what gives her, when confronted with the choice of betraying that love by trying to please a new master or earning his hatred by refusing to "give my heart to my new husband" (763/662), the inner strength to face the choice unflinchingly and reaffirm her loyalty to Hector. Hecuba, who urges the opposite course for the sake of a future she still believes may bring some good, remains, for all that she is overcome by fainting and grief as she absorbs the news of one disaster after another, a figure of astounding resilience. She is the fallen queen, of course, who not surprisingly laments all she has lost, but the secret of her strength appears to be the more ordinary emotions of a mother and grandmother, the fact that that she never loses sight of the loved ones who are left, never ceases to want the future to mitigate their sorrow. So she tries to protect Cassandra and, in the episode we have just been examining, to convince Andromache to make the best of her new circumstances. All her efforts are futile in the face of the terrible events that threaten to overwhelm her, but she will continue to struggle nonetheless, furiously debating Helen in the name of justice for Troy, gathering what gifts she can to give Astyanax his rites of burial. When at last she yields to despair, and even the attempt to end her life in the flames of her burning city is thwarted, she will rise once more and lead her women into their new lives, come what may.

Hecuba's resilience is shown in a different way in the episode that comes next. Once more, Euripides gives a new female character a striking entrance—not one of the Trojans this time, but Helen, the woman they most despise. Although she has been mentioned several times already, most notably in Andromache's bitter curse at the end of the last episode, we only learn that she will make an appearance in the play with the arrival of her husband Menelaus, who bursts into the deepening gloom to proclaim, "How gloriously bright the sun is shining" (994/860), now that he will lay hands on his treacherous wife at last. Helen is just another captive, given to him to do with what he will, and he has decided "to sail back to Greece with her / And kill her there" (1014–5/ 877–8). Hecuba responds with a strange, perhaps even bewildered apostrophe to Zeus as Air, or Mind, or Necessity of Nature.[28] The stasimon that followed Andromache's and Astyanax's departures ended on a note of despair: "the gods / Who loved Troy once love Troy no longer" (992–3/ 858–9), and Hecuba herself had called them "useless allies in a time of need" (549/469). Now, however, her novel invocation of the "boundless mystery / called Zeus" (1021–2/885–6) allows for the possibility of an inscrutable process that will set things right, that seems to promise the fulfillment of the one hope left to the Trojan women, albeit only the hope that whatever force controls Troy's destiny will at last wreak vengeance upon the first cause of Troy's ruin.

Hecuba tells Menelaus that he will win her praise if he kills Helen, but that he must avoid being ensnared by the power of Helen's glance and charms. However great Hecuba's hope, she remains alert to the danger that her enemy will yet escape unharmed. On this note, Helen herself enters, manhandled (or so she claims) by Menelaus's men, but nevertheless—as Hecuba will pointedly mention—"tricked out in all your finery" instead of appearing, as would be fitting, "in filthy rags / Your head shaved, trembling, humbled by fear" (1193–6/1022–6). These lines give us a crucial visual clue: Helen is as concerned as ever with appearances, a true votary of Aphrodite and a shrewd survivor, standing among the battered, ragged, gray band of Trojan woman, still radiantly beautiful, still alluring, still dangerous.

The episode is cast as a formal debate, with Menelaus in the role of judge. It is noteworthy that the debate begins, against all the rules of both law courts and stage trials, with the defense, even before the plaintiff has lodged charges. Helen immediately asks to speak; Menelaus does not wish to hear her, but Hecuba insists that Helen be allowed to defend herself, so much does she want to be sure that her enemy is confuted, so confident is she that her case will prevail.[29] At least for the original audience, however, this confidence would have carried a bitter irony, for they all surely knew that Helen would survive. Hecuba appears to have the upper hand, and this is the only scene of the play in which that is so, but spectators will have evaluated Menelaus's promise of future punishment in the light of a familiar scene in Book Four of the

---

28. For the philosophical background of this prayer, see the note on 1020–5.
29. On Hecuba's motivation, see also the note on 1047.

Odyssey.[30] There it is clear that he forgave his errant wife and settled back into his old life in Sparta with Helen at his side; we find them living together, if not in harmony, at least in mutual forbearance and a kind of brittle domesticity. We have no reason to think that Euripides expected his audience to change their minds about what happened to Helen, and there are hints in the scene that the announced decision will not stand.[31] The most obvious such suggestion comes at the end. Menelaus has heard both sides and reiterates that he will take Helen home for public stoning. When Hecuba warns him not to let her sail home on his ship, he replies with what we might least expect from this grim play—a joke: "Why not? Has she gained weight? Is she too heavy now?" (**1225**/1050).[32] So far is he from understanding her point, or so loath to admit that he has understood it!

Helen's erotic nature is central to the debate itself in other ways. The crux of Helen's argument is that it is not she, but rather Aphrodite, the goddess of love, who bears responsibility for her desertion of Menelaus and escape with Paris. Hecuba's reply "rationalizes" Helen's claim in a way that may well seem convincing to modern sensibilities: Aphrodite "is just the name we give to lust run wild" (**1148**/989). At the end of the debate, Menelaus echoes this sentiment by saying that Helen "invokes Aphrodite / As a smoke screen" (**1211–2**/1038–9). And yet, the power of Aphrodite inhabits this scene in so many ways. The element of "spectacle" that we

---

30. See in particular *Odyssey* 4.120–305.

31. These hints, however, should not be given undue weight. K. Lee, in his edition of the play (London, 1976), blunts the force of the contradiction between the formal outcome of the debate and the known myth by tacitly changing the outcome to fit the demands of the myth. "At the beginning [Menelaus] simulates severity, but gradually his real feelings become evident and by the end of the episode we are certain that his condemnation of Helen is only verbal" (219–20). When Menelaus will not speak Helen's name, he "is so concerned to give the impression" that he is done with her that he "descends to the childish" (221). Menelaus "protests too much" and "continues to pretend indifference" (243), and so on in a similar vein. This rough and ready psychologizing, though at a certain level not unwarranted, misrepresents the far subtler and more intriguing way in which Euripides manages the scene as a demonstration of the power of eros on the one hand and the failure of self-knowledge on the other. At the opposite end of the spectrum, however, the vigorous argument of M. Lloyd, *The Agon in Euripides* (Oxford, 1992), 99–112, to show that Euripides leaves the outcome of the debate deliberately uncertain also fails to account for the full effect of the episode. For Lloyd, the debate is about the Trojan War and is thus "too important to be tied down to the comparatively trivial question of whether Helen will be punished" (112). Lloyd takes Menelaus's protestations at face value and argues that the elements of the scene often taken to undercut his resolve—principally Hecuba's warnings—are not sufficient to establish that he will *not* punish her. But on one level, at least, the debate is precisely about whether Helen will be punished, and the audience's complicit awareness that she will not is absolutely crucial to its dramatic effect.

32. Justina Gregory, "Comic Elements in Euripides," *Illinois Classical Studies* 24–5 (1999–2000): 69–72, argues vigorously against taking this line as a joke, but in my view she misunderstands the nature of the exchange. To go no further, it need not be, as she claims, a "fat joke" of a kind for which we have no evidence from ancient Greece. (After all, Helen is standing there in all her overwhelming beauty.) The joke is not really about Helen; it is about Menelaus, who misses Hecuba's point entirely. Whether he does so intentionally, i.e., brushes her concern aside with the silly suggestion that his boat might become seriously overloaded if he took Helen aboard, or whether he simply reveals his utter incomprehension, his remark is amusing, and disturbingly so.

mentioned with regard to her costume earlier and that no doubt infuses every aspect of Helen's appearance—movements, gestures, vocal inflections—comes into its own in this scene, for it becomes the embodiment of a power that we know will reduce the proud general who stoutly resists it here to an ignominious capitulation. And indeed, we see the danger signs already, particularly through Hecuba's eyes.

It is not, of course, that Hecuba is simply wrong about Helen and has no good arguments to make, and it is certainly not that Helen's claims are to be taken at face value. But Hecuba's attempts at "demythologizing" Helen' story are fraught with a fundamental difficulty. The "beauty contest" on Mount Ida, for example, which Hecuba treats as an irrational absurdity, is part and parcel of the mythological foundation upon which the entire play is based, from Poseidon's recollection of building Troy's walls together with Apollo, in the first lines of the prologue, to the gods' disastrous loves for mortal Trojans, evoked in the stasimon that immediately precedes this episode. The most famous case of this sort in Euripides occurs at *Heracles* 1340–6, where the hero, newly recovered from an attack of madness in which he killed his wife and children, calls all the traditional tales of divine amours and other excesses "wretched lies of poets." He thereby summarily denies his own descent from Zeus, although the play itself has been at pains to prove his doubts about his divine parentage mistaken.

Such Euripidean provocations as these are part of a complex and grimly playful confrontation with the question of what the old tales really say about the place of humans in a mysterious and often hostile cosmos. The deities that Hecuba, strictly for the sake of refuting Helen, imagines as behaving rationally, in ways that humans can readily understand and approve, do not make sense in the larger context of the play but only as one gambit in a complex and unending search for meaning in the most extreme circumstances. In the episode we are examining, Euripides engages the complicity of his audience in an ironic, even deconstructive "reading" of the action as it unfolds before them. As the scene progresses in a kind of bitter deadpan to the apparent condemnation of Helen, the spectators' awareness of its incongruity with what they know permits them, with a minimum of hints and pointing, to construct a very different scene, one that enacts the undoing of what they are witnessing.

Euripides has designed this scene, in short, as a sort of self-consuming artifact (to borrow Stanley Fish's term from a different context).[33] It is a daring and quintessentially Euripidean technique that acknowledges both the overwhelming power and the moral inscrutability of the gods, or the irrational, or whatever we choose to call the forces that shape our fortunes.

---

33. Stanley E. Fish, *Self-Consuming Artifacts: The Experience of Seventeenth-Century Literature* (Berkeley and Los Angeles, 1972).

Menelaus is weak, but Euripides seems less interested in exposing his weakness than in illustrating the power of eros. The distinction is important. Critics stirred by Hecuba's passionate rhetoric have tended to accept at face value the assertion of human responsibility over divine responsibility, Hecuba's insistence that Aphrodite is just another name for lust, just an excuse for bad behavior. Such a conclusion seems far too simple, however, once we recognize how Euripides uses his spectators' knowledge of Helen's later life to engage them in thought. We confront the certainty of what Hecuba at this point can only fear—that Helen will escape punishment, that the Trojan women will get nothing, not even revenge.[34] If there is a just Zeus, his justice eludes Hecuba's calculus, and our own. Perhaps, as she insists, it is unjust that the gods should destroy a whole people over something so frivolous as a beauty contest; but what we are made to understand here about the insidious workings of beauty can hardly be called a demonstration that such a thing did not or could not happen. At any rate, the argument that Helen's lust alone caused Troy's downfall is paradoxically undermined by the power that eros exerts in this very scene. The demonstration of that power is all the more devastating for being so sly.

The Helen scene is cast as a rhetorical struggle, the only episode of *Trojan Women* that is conducted entirely in trimeter dialogue; there is no place in it for music of any kind. In the final movement of the play, however, centered as it is on rites of mourning and farewell, musical intensification of emotion is an essential ingredient. All that remains for the women of Troy to do is bury Astyanax and leave their city forever; the agitated rhythms of the lyrics combine with a series of powerful gestures to express the desperate urgency of their grief. Talthybius and his men return, bringing the dead child for burial, a small, shattered body laid out on the great shield of Hector, seen earlier among the spoils on Andromache's cart. Talthybius tells Hecuba with some tenderness that Andromache has already made a hasty, tearful departure, but only after she had obtained from her new master Neoptolemus permission to have her child buried with his father's shield for a coffin. The Greek herald entrusts Astyanax to his grandmother for funeral rites, adding that he has spared her the task of washing the child's body and cleansing his wounds by performing the task himself. The detail is telling: this is a duty normally entrusted to the nearest female relatives of the deceased, and Andromache, as he himself tells us, had asked for Hecuba to have charge of the preparations for burial. Talthybius's voluntary assistance comes as the culminating token of his increasing engagement with the sufferings of the women who have survived Troy's fall.

---

34. Compare the close of the following stasimon, where the Chorus pray that Menelaus not return home to Sparta "now that he's got back / The shame of Greece" (i.e., *Helen*, 1315–6/1114). The prayer in vain, as we know, and there is no further thought of any punishment for Helen.

Trojan Women has only two male characters: the weak and officious Menelaus, who appears in a single episode, bested, one might say, by both Helen and Hecuba; and this Greek herald, decent in a world of depravity and grief. Euripides has transformed the typically anonymous figure of the herald into a man of some sensitivity, whose role is not merely to bring the commands of his leaders to the enslaved women of Troy, but also to show us that even a Greek can see the horror those commands entail. We get some measure of the man from his first appearance, when he alludes to Polyxena's death with a series of almost delicate euphemisms: "She serves Achilles' tomb," "happy, free of trouble," "following her fate. Her cares are over" (291–7/264–71).[35] When he next returns, he expresses openly his anguish, even shame at the news he bears for Andromache from the beginning:

> Wife of Hector, once the bravest man
> In Troy, don't hate me for what I've come to tell you.
> Against my will, I must announce the common
> Will of the Greeks   (814–17/709–11).

There follows a hesitation that requires eight more lines of fraught exchange with Andromache before Talthybius can bring himself to announce that Astyanax is to be killed; as he himself says, "there's no easy way to tell the bad news" (824/717). At the end of the episode, having witnessed Andromache's horrified and despairing response to this new loss and given her the best advice he can, he leaves with the child, ruefully remarking that the man who does his job "ought to be all ruthlessness, / Someone with a heart more shameless than mine" (904–5/787–9). By the end of the play, as we have seen, Talthybius offers Hecuba and her companions the only help he can. He is of course still a Greek; he has a realistic grasp of what has happened and why, and he is understandably eager to begin the trip home. For all that, Euripides has gone out of his way to emphasize Talthybius's humanity in a world seemingly bereft of that quality, and in a way that makes the inhumanity of the Greeks' treatment of Troy's survivors all the more repugnant.[36]

---

35. To gauge the tone of these double entendres, cf. Euripides' *Hecuba* 989, where Hecuba asks for and receives a similar (though far less equivocal) assurance that her son Polydorus is alive and well from Polymestor, the very man who killed him. The spectators know that this response is both deceitful and self-interested. Here, Talthybius avoids an out-and-out lie (Hecuba speaks of his "riddling words" when she hears the truth from Andromache), and his motive can only be understood as some combination of sympathy and shame.

36. Commentators sometimes offer surprisingly harsh assessments of Talthybius's character. K. Lee, in the introduction to his edition (xxiv–v), while allowing that Talthybius has been "drawn with great skill," thinks the main feature of his character is "self-importance and pride in the grandeur of Hellas; he can scarcely think of anything else." Despite his sympathy for the women's lot, he has "no understanding of the tragedy which he witnesses" and is "without a will of his own." It is hard to see how such a view of this character can be justified. For a more balanced assessment, see K. Gilmartin, "Talthybius in the *Trojan Women*," *American Journal of Philology* 91 (1970): 213–22.

After Talthybius's departure, Hecuba first delivers what is in effect a funeral oration over her grandson, a brilliant substitute for a conventional messenger speech describing the boy's death.[37] Her address to the young Astyanax's broken body, evoking once more what might have been, recalling his loving words and gestures, is almost unbearable in its intimacy. The funeral rites conclude with a *kommos* in which Hecuba receives from her attendants such robes and ornaments as they have been able to find, and she adorns the child laid out upon his father's shield, continuing to address him in spoken iambics while the Chorus sing their anguished lament and beat their heads in mourning. The improvised ceremony completed, Hecuba bids the attendants carry Astyanax away for burial.

Talthybius returns to announce that Troy is being put to the torch and that the women must move to the ships. After one last, desolate apostrophe to Troy and to the gods she knows are not listening, Hecuba breaks at last and tries to die with her city by rushing into the flames. Talthybius stops her and puts her into the hands of his men, who are to take her to her new master, Odysseus. It is a moment of great poignancy, but not Hecuba's last. She does not go meekly, but leads the Chorus in a final *kommos*, a lyric lament of staggering intensity. With it, the play comes to a close; as Francis Dunn points out, this is the only play of Euripides to end in a lyric meter, and there is no "moral," no generalizing comment of any kind.[38] Once we have reached this pitch of disaster, what remains to be said? Hecuba falls to the ground one last time to beat the earth with her fists, and the Chorus follow suit in an extraordinary gesture of farewell to—and solidarity with—their beloved dead, but above all in a call to witness. Then, as they hear the wall of Troy collapse, Hecuba rises one last time, orders her trembling limbs to carry her into slavery, and leads the Trojan women slowly but without stumbling toward the ship. There could be no more fitting final vision of Hecuba, against all odds the embodiment of human fortitude in the midst of despair.

PETER BURIAN

---

37. See also the note on 1366–1422.

38. Dunn (above, n. 17), 102. In other extant tragedies of Euripides, the Chorus chant the closing lines in marching anapests (trochaic tetrameters in *Ion*).

ON THE TRANSLATION

Down three games to zero in the 2004 American League Championship best-of-seven series, the Boston Red Sox beat the New York Yankees four straight times to win the Pennant. The Red Sox became the first team in any sport to win a series after losing the first three games. When asked how they overcame that deficit, Terry Francona, the Boston manager, said they tried to narrow their focus from winning the series, or even winning each game, to winning each inning, each at bat, each pitch. By breaking down the series into games, the games into innings, and the innings into at bats and pitches, the BoSox established small, achievable goals. As a result, he said, they were never overwhelmed by the enormity of the challenge they faced.

Francona's strategy aptly describes how I went about translating *The Trojan Women*. First of all, I had to forget who it was I was translating. I had to forget that Euripides is one of the greatest poet/playwrights who ever lived, and that of all the surviving tragedies, *The Trojan Women* is perhaps the purest, and most heart-wrenching expression of the tragic spirit—undeserved and unredemptive suffering. I also had to forget that by and large tragic language is, in John Herrington's words, "a distinct and easily recognizable composite genre-dialect...a dialect which was never spoken outside the theatre but was mostly as remote from the language of the streets as the tragic masks and costumes were from the dress of the streets." I narrowed my focus to each sentence, each line, each word. Of course, my situation differed from the situation facing the Red Sox in that from the outset I knew I was going to lose. What I attempted to do, what I hoped to do, was to lose in an interesting and responsible way, in a way that honored my opponent by dramatizing my own intimate understanding of his unique achievement. I took to heart Cervantes' complaint that reading a translation is "like looking at the Flanders Tapestries from behind: you can see the basic shapes, but they are so filled with threads that you cannot fathom their original luster."

In this translation, I try to fathom, if not to preserve, the original luster of *The Trojan Women*. Relying on Shirley Barlow's prose translation, I cast the spoken passages in blank verse, and the choral and monodic odes in a variety of two- to four-beat accentual lines. I use blank verse because of its flexibility, its capaciousness, and its potential to modulate subtly between formal and informal levels of speech. Blank verse can heighten into lyricism of intense emotion or accommodate and dramatize the rhetorical flourishes of argumentation. It can feel thoughtfully, and think feelingly. To avoid monotony, I vary degrees of stress among accented and unaccented syllables, I substitute anapestic and trochaic feet for iambs here and there, and I play the phrases off against the lines while making sure the line cuts into the sentence at relatively stable places, so that the line itself never ceases to be heard, even while the volume of it as a measure, as and a pattern of sound, is constantly changing. The shorter accentual lines of the odes reflect the intensification of feeling, as do the denser imagery and the forward lilt of the sentences, mimicking both the accelerating sense of doom and the struggle to preserve a sense of dignity in the face of catastrophic loss and suffering.

My poetry, of course, is not as rich or intricate as Euripides'. There is simply no way to bring his complex music over into English. The amalgamation of lyric meters in *The Trojan Women*, each with its own particular conventions and tonal associations, is impossible to replicate. All I hoped to do is to find some metrical and stylistic analogies for untranslatable effects. What I offer here is an intimate, creative reading of one poetry by another, a reading that I hope reveals and honors the emotional and verbal richness of the primary text. The most that any translator can hope for is to fail in ways that send the reader back to the original with a freshened sense of how unbeatably wonderful it is.

ALAN SHAPIRO

TROJAN WOMEN

CHARACTERS

POSEIDON god of the sea

ATHENA warrior goddess

HECUBA Queen of Troy, now enslaved

CHORUS of captive Trojan women

TALTHYBIUS herald of the Greek army

CASSANDRA daughter of Hecuba and King Priam

ANDROMACHE widow of Hector, mother of Astyanax

MENELAUS Greek general, husband of Helen

HELEN Spartan daughter of Zeus and Leda, wife of Menelaus,
then of Paris

Mute roles:

ASTYANAX son of Hector and Andromache

SERVANTS and ARMED ATTENDANTS

The scene is an open space outside the wall of the captured city of Troy. The stage building represents the walls of the city, and against the walls are perhaps three huts or tents that house the captured women who are the sole survivors of the defeated city. QUEEN HECUBA, now a slave, with hair shorn and dressed in rags, is helped by other captive women, similarly attired, from the central hut to the center of the stage, where she collapses. After a brief pause, POSEIDON enters, either atop the walls of the city or from a side entrance.

POSEIDON I am Poseidon. I come from the deep brine
Of the Aegean where the Nereids dance
In circling choruses on faultless feet.
Ever since the day that Phoebus Apollo
And I with straight rule set down the enclosing
Towers and stone walls in this Trojan land,
My heart has loved these Phrygians and their city.
But now the city smolders, toppled, sacked
By Argive spears. Pallas Athena willed
What Epeius devised, the man from Phocis   10
Where Parnassus looms — a brood mare big with
    weapons
To send inside the city walls, heavy
With death, which men of later times will call
The Wooden Horse whose belly hid the spears.
The sacred groves are now deserted, and blood
Oozes from the temples of the gods.
Priam lies cut down by the steps that rise
To the altar of Zeus, protector of the hearth.
Pile on pile of gold and Trojan plunder
Is being dragged away to the Greek ships.   20
And now, after ten long years, the Greeks who crushed
This city are only waiting for the right wind,
A favoring wind to bring them home at last
To the great joy of holding wives and children
In their arms, of seeing those longed-for faces.

Hera, the Argive goddess, and Athena
Joined forces to destroy the Trojans and
Defeat me too, so I'm deserting Troy,

Leaving this famous city and my altars here.
For when desolation seizes a town,   30
Religion falters, the gods receive no honor.
Cry echoes cry down Scamander's stream,
The cry of women suddenly enslaved,
Soon to be divvied up to masters: some
To the Arcadians, some to the Thessalians,
And others to the sons of Theseus,
The royalty of Athens. Here in this tent
The still-unchosen Trojan women wait,
The ones the generals have set aside
Just for themselves, and among them is one   40
Rightly treated as a captive slave,
The daughter of Tyndareus, Helen of Sparta.

(POSEIDON *points to the fallen figure at the center of the
stage.*)

But there is Hecuba, if anyone cares to see her,
Unhappy woman face down before the door,
Weeping her many tears for many reasons.
Her daughter Polyxena was killed at Achilles' tomb,
Mercilessly, though she doesn't know it yet.
Priam, her husband, is dead. Her sons are dead.
Her one remaining child, Cassandra, maddened
By Apollo's touch and made untouchable,   50
Will soon be forced to sleep in Agamemnon's
Unholy bed. Taking her, he spurns
Lord Apollo's will and all piety.
O city that flourished once within your towers,
Your high stone walls, farewell. If Zeus's daughter,
Pallas Athena, hadn't destroyed you, you
Would still be standing firm on firm foundations.

ATHENA *enters and joins* POSEIDON.

ATHENA   May I put aside the bad blood between us
And speak now to my father's close relation,
Whose awesome power is honored among the gods?   60

POSEIDON   Of course. The ties of blood, Lady Athena,
Irresistibly charm the mind and heart.

ATHENA   I thank you for your kindness. I want to raise
         A subject that concerns us both, my lord.

POSEIDON Has a new directive been sent out
         From Zeus, or one of the other gods?

ATHENA   No, it's for Troy's sake, where we are standing now,
         That I would win your power to my side.

POSEIDON But has your hatred given way to pity
         Now that fire has burned the city down to ash?   70

ATHENA   Let's keep to the subject. Will you advise me,
         Help me accomplish what I want to do?

POSEIDON Of course I will. But tell me what it is
         You want, and on whose behalf—the Greeks
                  or Trojans?

ATHENA   I want to help the Trojans whom I've hated
         And hurt the Greek troops as they journey home.

POSEIDON Why does your mind blow with the winds of chance
         Too much this way or that, in love or hate?

ATHENA   You've heard how they insulted me, my temples?

POSEIDON Yes—when Ajax dragged Cassandra off by force.   80

ATHENA   And the Greeks said nothing, did nothing, they just
                  looked on.

POSEIDON And yet you gave them the strength to conquer Troy.

ATHENA   That's why, with your help, I would make them suffer.

POSEIDON I'll gladly help. But what do you want to do?

ATHENA   Make their homecoming a coming home to pain.

POSEIDON Right here on land, or on the open sea?

ATHENA   At sea, while they are sailing home from Troy.
          Zeus will unleash an avalanche of rain
          And pummeling hail and gale storms black as night.
          He's promised to let me hurl his thunderbolt   90
          Against the Greeks, to blast their ships to nothing,
          But as for you, your task is the Aegean sea,
          To roil it up with towering waves and whirlpools
          Till Euboea's deep bay churns with corpses,
          So that from now on Greeks will learn to revere
          My awesome power, and honor all the gods.

POSEIDON Consider it done. What you've asked me to do
          Needs only doing, not long speeches. I'll rouse
          The Aegean waters until the shores of Mykonos,
          The jagged reefs of Delos, Skyros, Lemnos,   100
          And the promontories of Caphereus
          Are clogged with countless bodies. Go to Olympus,
          And when you aim your father's thunderbolts,
          Watch for the moment when the Greeks set sail.
          The man who sacks cities, who desecrates temples
          And graves, the holy places of the dead,
          That man's a fool. For all his pillaging,
          Sooner or later, his own destruction comes.

              POSEIDON *and* ATHENA *leave the stage; after another mo-*
              mentary pause, HECUBA *raises her head and begins to sing.*

HECUBA   You wretch, lift up your head,
          Lift it up off the ground. Look up: 110
          The Troy before you is no longer Troy,
          The queen of Troy is queen no longer.
              This is the changing fortune
          You must bear. Bear it. Sail
          With the hard current of the strait,
              Sail with destiny,
          Don't steer your life's prow back
              Into the heaving waves;
          Sail as you do, and have, and will
          On the winds of chance. *AIAI. AIAI.*   120
          What's not to mourn for in my misery—
          My homeland gone, my children gone,
              My husband? And you, too,

Ancestral glory, all that opulence,
You added up to what? To nothing.
   So why be silent now?
And yet, why not be silent? Why sing
   A dirge? What good can it do?
Unlucky as I am, my limbs
So beaten down that they can only   130
Lie here on this hard bed crushed beneath
The crushing weight of destiny.
   From head, from temple
Down to ribs, oh how my body
Longs to rock on waves of grief, the spine-
   Keel tilting side to side,
In rhythm to this long lament,
   These tears, the only music
Left for the wretched, singing the song
Of troubles no one dances to.   140

And you, you prows of ships with quickened oars
That skimmed the blue waves to holy Troy,
   Out past the beautiful,
Calm harbors of Greece, and while the war
Song of your hateful flutes was sounding,
   And the melodious pipes
Were playing hatefully, you dropped
   Your anchors with Egyptian cable
Off the Trojan shore, hunting
The hateful wife of Menelaus,   150
Her brother Castor's blight, the shame
Of the Eurotas, she who killed Priam,
   Father of fifty sons,
Who made me, wretched Hecuba,
Founder against the reef she is.
Look where I've come to, where I sit,
Here by the tents of Agamemnon.
   Look how bereft of home
I am, a slave, an old woman slave,
My head shaved to the very bone.   160
   Troy burns, swallowed up in flame:
You pitiable wives of bronze-
   Speared Trojan warriors—
You daughters wed to ruin, come,

Let us keen for Troy, and like
A mother bird for her fallen chicks, I'll cry
The loudest, though my song is not the song
   I led once, honoring
The gods, my footsteps beating out
The frank praise of the dance while Priam,   170
Smiling, leaned on his scepter.

Half of the CHORUS *enters from a hut at one side of the stage.*

HALF-CHORUS 1 Hecuba, why the shrill cries you cry?   *Strophe*
Where will your outburst take us? Even from
Inside the tent I heard you keening.
Your pitiful wail sent fear cutting through us,
Right through the hearts of Trojan women
Mourning indoors their day of bondage.

HECUBA The oarsmen of the Greeks are stirring;
See how they're moving to the ships.

HALF-CHORUS 1 Is this their will? Has the time come   180
To tear me from my ancestral home?

HECUBA I don't know. I only guess our ruin.

HALF-CHORUS 1 *(turning to call their companions still inside)*
Ah, you unlucky Trojans, come out
And hear the harsh toils
You'll soon be caught in. The Greeks
Are getting ready to go home.

HECUBA Ah, wait, don't let Cassandra out,
Crazed and delirious, for the Argives
To mock, as if the pain I feel
Weren't sharp enough already.   190
Ah Troy, unlucky, unhappy Troy,
Your time is over now, and those
Who leave you are unhappy too,
The living and the dead alike.

The second half of the CHORUS *enters from a hut at the other
side of the stage.*

HALF-CHORUS 2 Trembling in an icy sweat, I've rushed?   *Antistrophe*
From Agamemnon's tents to hear you,
My queen. The Argives, have they decided
To kill me, wretched creature that I am?
Or are the sailors poised to seize
The oars and set the ships in motion?   200

HECUBA My child, I awoke at dawn, my spirit
Wracked with panic, terrified.

HALF-CHORUS 2 Has the Greek herald come already?
Whose wretched chattel am I to be?

HECUBA We'll learn that any moment now.

HALF-CHORUS 2 Who'll take me—Argive or Phthian?
Will I, poor wretch, be going to
Some island far away from Troy?

HECUBA O god, O god, whose slave shall I be?
Where in this wide world shall I live   210
My life out, doing drudgework,
Stooped, mechanical, a less-than-
Feeble token of the dead?
Shall I be a guard, stationed at
Their doors? A nursemaid to their children?
I who was once the queen of Troy?

CHORUS AIAI, our ruined lives, this brutal outrage—
What dirges you could sing!
Never again to lead the whirling shuttle
Over and back across   220
Our Trojan looms. Never again
To see our parents' home.
I see it for the last time now
And know that I have even
Greater suffering in store—
Dragged to some Greek's bed
(Oh, I dread that night, that fated dark)
Or bent under the weight
Of water I'll be forced to draw
At Peirene's sacred fountain.   230

If the choice were mine, I'd choose
    The land of Theseus,
So blessed and famous, but not, no,
    Never for a moment,
The swirling river of Eurotas,
    Detested home of Helen,
Where I'd have to lower my eyes
    To Menelaus,
Scourge of Troy. Word too has reached me
    Of Peneus's hallowed ground,   240
Glittering navel stone of Mount
    Olympus, dense with fruits
And riches, and where I would go
    If I couldn't go
To Theseus's holy land.
    I've also heard the land
Of Etna, stronghold of Hephaestus,
    Across the sea from Carthage, is
Renowned for the garlands it has won.
    And I've heard there's another   250
Country, near the Ionian Sea,
    That the shining river Crathis
Nurtures with water so blessed it dyes
    The hair of those who bathe
Red gold, and makes the men
    Of that place strong and happy.

           TALTHYBIUS *enters from the side, accompanied by armed*
                                  soldiers.

Look over there—here comes a herald
    From the Greek army.
What news is he bringing in such haste?
    What's left to say?   260
We already know we're slaves to Greece.

TALTHYBIUS Hecuba, I can call you by your name
              Because I've come so often as a herald
              From the Greek camp. I'm Talthybius.
              Surely you know me from the times before.
              I've come again with news for all of you.

HECUBA   *AIAI*! It's come at last, dear friends, what we have feared.

TALTHYBIUS   If what you've feared is your assigned lots, yes.

HECUBA   Is it Thebes, dear god, or some Thessalian city?

TALTHYBIUS   You've each been given to a separate master.   270

HECUBA   Who is given to whom? And who among us now,
Which Trojan woman, will find happiness?

TALTHYBIUS   I know, I'll tell you, but you have to ask
The questions one by one, not all at once.

HECUBA   My daughter, my poor girl Cassandra, tell me, then—
Who's taken her? Who's she been given to?

TALTHYBIUS   King Agamemnon picked her for his prize.

HECUBA   A queen's child—to be a slave to that Spartan queen!
Gods! How could my misery get any worse?

TALTHYBIUS   No, no, not a slave, but a mistress, a bedmate.   280

HECUBA   Cassandra, Apollo's virgin, she to whom the gold-
Haired god has given the gift of never marrying?

TALTHYBIUS   Desire for the god-seized girl cut deep.

HECUBA   My child, my child, hurl down your holy laurel branches,
And strip your body of the sacred wreaths you wear.

TALTHYBIUS   Yes, she'll attain a king's bed. What could be better?

HECUBA   And what of the child you took from me, my little girl?
Where is my youngest? What have you done with her?

TALTHYBIUS   Do you mean Polyxena, or someone else?

HECUBA   Yes, Polyxena. Her fate has bound her to whom?   290

TALTHYBIUS   She serves Achilles' tomb—that's the decree.

HECUBA   She? Guarding a tomb? Ah! A child I bore!
      What's this, my friend? Some law established long ago?
      Something decreed by custom among the Greeks?

TALTHYBIUS   Think of your daughter as happy, free of trouble.

HECUBA   What do you mean, she's "happy"? Is she still alive?

TALTHYBIUS   She's following her fate. Her cares are over.

HECUBA   And the wife of Hector, fierce in arms, Andromache,
      That poor girl, what befalls her now? With whom?

TALTHYBIUS   Achilles' son has picked her for his prize.   300

HECUBA   And what of my fate? Whom will I serve, with
        my gnarled
      Hand on the stick I cannot walk without?

TALTHYBIUS   Odysseus, Lord of Ithaca. You'll be his slave.

HECUBA   *AIAI.* Not this!
      Tear the shorn head,
      Rip cheeks with nails,
        Wail, scream,
      My luck is to serve
        The foulest man
      Alive, back stabber,   310
        Justice hater,
      Hell-born snake
        Whose slick tongue
      Twists everything
        To nothing, twists
      Love to hate,
        And hate to love.
      Weep for me,
        Trojan women,
      Weep for this wretched   320
        Fate. I am gone.
      The worst of all
        Possible lots is mine.

CHORUS LEADER Your fate is known, my lady. But what of mine,
               Who'll be my master? What Achaean,
                    what Greek?

TALTHYBIUS You servants, quick, go inside and get Cassandra,
            So I can turn her over to the commander,
            Then divvy up the other women prisoners
            To the officers who drew their names.

                    (The attendants stop short, and TALTHYBIUS *points at the
                    central hut.)*

                                          What now?
            Some torch flame bursting from inside the tent?   330
            The Trojan women, frantic, soon to be torn
            From home—have they set their rooms on fire?
            Or have they set fire to themselves, burning
            Themselves to death, the way free spirits do
            Who find bad luck like this unbearable?
            Open those doors—right now—right away. I fear
            That what they want to do will rile the Greeks,
            And I'll get blamed.

HECUBA   There is no fire. No one
            Is burning anything. It's just my daughter,
            Cassandra, delirious, running out to us.   340

                    CASSANDRA *enters, dancing out of the central hut with a
                    flaming torch in each hand and singing a lyric monody.*

CASSANDRA See how I lift the torch,   *Strophe*
               How I wave it, whirl with it—
           How my reverence for this sacred
           Precinct flares—
               O Lord Hymenaeus!

           Hymen, how blessed the bridegroom,
               How blessed the bride,
           Blessed by a royal wedding, soon,
           At Argos—
               O Hymen, Lord   350

41

Hymenaeus! And mother,
　　While you weep, keening,
Day and night for my dead father
And our beloved
　　Country,

It falls to me to set
　　The torch fires blazing
At my own wedding, to make them blaze
In a wheel
　　Of radiance   360

That lights the way for you,
　　Hymenaeus,
And you, Hecate, as is the custom
For a young girl's
　　Marriage.

Step high and lead the dance —   *Antistrophe*
　　Euhan! Euhoi! —
Just as we did before in glad times
When my father
　　Lived.   370

The dance is sacred. You lead
　　The dance, Apollo,
You lead it as I, crowned with bay leaves,
Offer sacrifice
　　In your temple.

Hymen, O Hymenaeus!
　　And you, mother,
You, too, lead the dance, join in it
Joyously,
　　And turning   380

As I turn, now here, now there,
　　Sing out
The wedding song, yes, celebrate
The bride
　　With blessed chants

And clapping hands. Come,
  Trojan daughters,
In all your finery, sing for the husband
Fate has chosen
  I lie down beside.   390

CHORUS LEADER   My queen, can't you calm her delirium
                Before she dances off lightly to the Greek camp?

HECUBA   O Hephaestus, holder of the wedding torch,
         The torch you hold here burns with misery,
         The opposite of all I ever hoped for.
         I never dreamed, my child, that you'd be married
         At spear point, forced into marriage by Greek arms.
         Hand me the torch. Child, hand it to me now,
         In your mad rush you're carrying it wrong,
         It isn't straight. *(gently taking one torch from* CASSANDRA)
                      These new trials haven't shocked you   400
         Into sanity but left you as you were.
         Women of Troy, come take away the torches,
         And let's replace her wedding songs with tears.

         (Women take both torches, and CASSANDRA *resumes in spoken
                                                          verse.)*

CASSANDRA   Mother, enwreathe my head; crown it with triumph.
            Rejoice! I'm marrying a king. Escort me,
            And if you think I'm dragging my feet, push me,
            Force me forward, for if Loxias
            Is still Loxias, the great Greek leader,
            Agamemnon, marrying me, will make
            A marriage more disastrous than Helen's.   410
            Our wedding night will be a night of death
            And devastation for his house; I'll kill him, I'll
            Avenge my father and my brothers' blood.
            But let all that go! Enough! Why should I
            Sing about the blade that's soon to slash
            My throat, and the throat of others, or how my marriage
            Will set the plot in motion to butcher a mother
            And bring down the house of Atreus?
                                    I may be mad,
            God-seized, but I will stand outside my madness

Enough to show you how much luckier   420
Our city's lot is than the Greeks'. Consider:
For just one woman's sake, one fit of passion,
The Greeks tracked Helen down and slaughtered thousands.
Consider too how clever he was, the general
Who slaughtered what he loved for what he hated,
Sacrificing the sweetness of his child
At home to his brother, for one woman's sake,
A woman who wasn't taken off by force
But went freely. And when the Greeks came at last
To the Scamander, all along its banks   430
They were cut down, one after another,
Though no one had been menacing their homeland,
Raiding their borders, scaling their high-walled cities.
And those the War God caught never again
Got to see their children, nor had their bodies wrapped
In winding sheets by their wives' hands.
They all lie buried in a foreign land
While at home it goes no better, for their wives
Die widows, and their parents childless,
The old who raised their children up for what?   440
So there would be nobody to tend their tombs
With offerings of blood?
                              (This is the praise
Their army's earned. Silence better suits
Such shamefulness. I'd never want my muse
To be a singer of nothing but disaster.)

Now think about the Trojans. Consider how
They have by far the greater glory: they died
Defending their homeland. And those the spear cut
          down
Were carried home by loved ones who by right
Prepared the corpses for burial and buried them   450
In their ancestral earth's embrace. And those
Who fought and lived found comfort day by day
At day's end with their wives and children, pleasures
The Greeks no longer knew.
                                   And even Hector,
You think his fate so terrible and cruel?
Listen, the truth is, though he's dead and gone,
He wouldn't be the Hector that he is

To all the world now if the Greeks had stayed home.
If they had not invaded, who would have known
Or seen how brave he was? And Paris too —   460
Whom would he have married? Not Zeus's daughter,
But some nameless wife!
                  All sane men think
A war of choice is madness for a city,
But when war's forced upon you, to die a hero
Wreathes your city's reputation in glory,
While to die a coward smears the city with shame.
There is no need, then, mother, to shed tears
For our country or my marriage. By marrying,
I'll kill the very ones I hate the most.

CHORUS LEADER You're giddy at your own calamities,   470
               Brightly singing what your song keeps dark.

TALTHYBIUS If Apollo hadn't made you crazy,
               We'd punish you for hurling at our leaders
               Such evil omens as they leave your country.
               But those called high and mighty are in the end
               The same as anyone. For the great Greek king,
               Beloved son of Atreus, has yoked
               Himself to a passion for this lunatic,
               While I, poor man that I am, would never leave
               My sandals by *her* bed.
                         Mad woman, I scatter   480
               Your Greek rants and Trojan praises to the winds.
               Follow me to the ships, a perfect bedmate
                For our wise leader. And you, Hecuba, you too
               Go willingly when Laertes' son arrives.
               For everyone who comes to Ilium says
               She's a good woman, his wife whose slave you'll be.

CASSANDRA This servant is too clever for his own good.
               Why do we flatter them with the name of "herald"
               When the whole world hates them, knows they're
                    nothing but
               Factotums, lackeys, lapdogs of tyrants and states?   490
               You say my mother will go to Odysseus's palace.
               And yet Apollo in his own words told me
               She'll die right here at home. I won't say more.

Why should I reproach her with the rest?
Odysseus, though, the fool, he thinks his trials
Are over. But what's in store for him will make
My suffering and the suffering of Troy
Seem like a paradise by comparison.
After ten years here, he won't come home
For ten more years—he'll have to face the whirling   500
Terror of Charybdis in the narrow strait,
And the moody mountain-dwelling Cyclops
Who rips flesh raw from the bone, and Circe,
The Ligurian witch, who turns men into pigs,
And he'll be shipwrecked too in the heaving sea,
And feel desire for the lotus, and hear the bloody
Flesh of the sacred Oxen of the Sun
Sizzle an unholy, sickening sound.
He'll go into the underworld alive
And after troubles on the sea, he'll find   510
His home infested with even more troubles.

But what's the point of hurling prophecies
About Odysseus's sorrows? It's time
To marry my bridegroom in the house of death.
Dishonorable man, they'll bury you
Dishonorably by night, in darkness, you,
Illustrious commander of the Greeks
Who brag of having brought Troy to its knees.
And me they'll slash and dump in some ravine
Where runoff from the rain will wash my corpse   520
Out by the grave of my beloved bridegroom,
And there I'll lie, naked, for wild beasts to feed on,
Me, the faithful servant of Apollo.

(CASSANDRA *removes her priestly headbands.*)

Farewell, you fillets of the god I loved
So well, you emblems of awe. I've left for good
The festivals in which I so rejoiced.
O lord of prophecy, see how they go,
Ripped from my body, my still untainted body,
How I scatter them to the winds for you, O lord.
Where's the king's ship? Where do I get on board?   530
We can't too quickly find a wind to fill

The sails, and when you take me from this land
You'll take with you a Fury, one of three.

Mother, goodbye. Don't cry. O my beloved
Country, and my brothers in the world below—
Soon you and our father will welcome me among you
When I've brought down the ruinous house of Atreus
And sink triumphant to the sunken dead.

CASSANDRA *is taken away by* TALTHYBIUS, *and* HECUBA *falls to
the ground grief-stricken.*

CHORUS LEADER   Caretakers of our aged Hecuba,
                Can't you see your mistress sprawled on the ground,   540
                Not saying anything, not even groaning?
                How can you let someone so old, so venerable,
                Just lie there? Lift her, you wretches, lift her up.

HECUBA   No, women, leave me lying where I've fallen.
         An unwanted kindness is no kindness at all.
         Is it any wonder I should faint
         From all I suffer and have suffered, and
         For all the suffering still to come? O gods!
         You useless allies in a time of need,
         And yet we're helpless not to call on them   550
         Whenever trouble strikes. *(rises slowly)*
                         But let me sing
         Of happier times one final time, so that
         My old good luck intensifies your pity
         For my bad luck now. I was a queen once,
         I married royalty, and I had royal sons,
         Supreme among all the Phrygians, sons such as
         No Trojan or Greek or any other foreign
         Mother could ever brag of having. And I,
         I had to watch them, son by son, brought down
         By the Greek spear, and for every one of them   560
         I cut my hair in mourning at their tombs.
         I wept for their father, Priam, not from hearing
         That he was butchered at the household altar—
         I saw with my own eyes. I saw firsthand
         The city overrun and torched. I saw
         The hands of strangers take my daughters,

Daughters I reared for husbands we would choose,
But I raised them only to be stolen from me,
Daughters, the daughters I'll never see again,
Who'll never see their mother. I am no mother,   570
But a slave, an old woman slave at that,
And—miserable capstone to all my misery—
Soon to be brought to Greece, where I'll be yoked
To work no woman my age should have to do.
What will I be, a servant at the door?
Keeper of the keys? I, the mother of Hector?
What will I do? Bake bread, then lay my bent
Back on the ground, far from the soft sheets
Of my royal bed, my raw flesh dressed in rags,
I who once wore luxurious robes? O god,   580
How miserable I am. Look at the misery
I've suffered and will go on suffering,
And why? Because of what? One woman's marriage?

Cassandra, my daughter, you breathed your
        inspiration
From the gods, but now on what humiliating
Bed will you have lost your purity?
And you, poor Polyxena, where are you?
So many children, and not a single one,
Not one of them, is left to ease my pain.
Yet you would help me to my feet? For what?   590
What's left to hope for? Guide my shackled steps
That glided once so easily through Troy.
Lead me to the straw mat on the ground,
The pillow of heaped stones where I'll lie down
And cry myself into oblivion.
Never mind how rich a man may be,
Don't call him lucky till he's dead and gone.

CHORUS Sing, Muse, sing of Ilium;   *Strophe*
        Sing full of tears a death song
            In a new key,   600
        In a strange key, for I will sing
        An ode for Troy, about my own destruction,
        How I was made a wretched slave
            By the four-wheeled horse
        The Argives left there at the gate,
        By the hidden thunder of spears inside it,

Fine harness of gold
Lightning all along its cheeks.

Our people on the Trojan rock,
Rejoicing, shouted, "Our troubles are over.   610
    Go bring the idol
Inside the walls to honor our Trojan goddess,
Zeus's daughter, go get it now!"
And who among us, what young girl
    Or old man didn't run
From their houses to sing and dance
Around the horse in their
    Enchantment
At their own death in disguise.

And all the Trojan people,   *Antistrophe*   620
All of us, swelled to the gates,
    To bring the gleaming
Treachery of mountain pinewood
To the goddess, a gift of Troy's destruction
For the virgin goddess of the deathless horses.
    And the crowd parted
Before the looming hull of that ship,
The country's death ship,
    Tugged by bright ropes
To the stone floor of Athena's temple.   630

And when at last night's blackness
Fell over their jubilant work,
    The Libyan flute
Played Trojan melodies
While girls lifted their feet
In joyous dance, and joyously
Raised their voices in song.
    And later, at home,
The blaze of flickering torch-fires
    Cast a gleam   640
Through the darkness of happy sleep.

And I too sang in the palace, sang   *Epode*
And danced in honor of Artemis,
The mountain-dwelling daughter of Zeus.
Then suddenly everywhere throughout the city

The same blood-
Soaked cry as children cowered behind their mothers,
    Trembling, clutching
Their mother's dresses, their only shield,
    As War came stalking from his hiding place.   650
The handiwork of Pallas—Trojans
Butchered at the altars, husbands
    Beheaded on the desolate beds
From which the wives were taken
To bear sons for Greece,
Troy's last humiliating pain.

> ANDROMACHE *enters with her son* ASTYANAX *on a cart piled*
> *high with Trojan spoils.*

Hecuba, look over there, do you see her—
Andromache on an enemy cart,
Astyanax, Hector's loved boy, held
To her panting breast? Poor woman,   660
Where are they taking you,
Jarred in the wagon by the bronze gear
Of Hector and the spear-caught Trojan
Spoils that Achilles' son will hang
In Phthia's temples, far from Troy?

ANDROMACHE The Greeks, our masters, are taking me away.

HECUBA *OIMOI.*

ANDROMACHE You cry my cry...

HECUBA *AIAI*...

ANDROMACHE ...for these afflictions...

HECUBA O Zeus!

ANDROMACHE ...for this hard fate.

HECUBA O, my children...

ANDROMACHE ...once—but now no more.   670

HECUBA   Our Troy, our power, lost, all lost...

ANDROMACHE   Miserably!

HECUBA   ...and all my high-born children...

ANDROMACHE   God, O God...

HECUBA   ...and all my...

ANDROMACHE   ...sorrows.

HECUBA   Pity our city's...

ANDROMACHE   ...destiny...

HECUBA   ...now sunk in smoke.

ANDROMACHE   Come back, my husband...

HECUBA   My son's a shade, my child,
It's to a shade you cry...

ANDROMACHE   ...protect me.
Scourge of the Greeks...   680

HECUBA   Firstborn of Priam's sons—
Who once were mine.

ANDROMACHE   I want to die,
I can't control this longing...

HECUBA   This is our fate, sad one, this anguish...

ANDROMACHE   ...for my lost city...

HECUBA   Pain crushes pain.

ANDROMACHE   ...because the gods hate us,
Your son eluded death and in a cursed bed
Brought down Troy's towers. And now
The mangled blood-soaked bodies lie

Sprawled at the feet of Pallas Athena   690
For the vultures to carry, piece by piece, away.
Your son—Paris, alone—yoked Troy to slavery.

HECUBA O my homeland, my unhappy homeland...

ANDROMACHE I weep for you, abandoned.

HECUBA ...you see your bitter end come round at last.

ANDROMACHE And I weep too for the house
Where I bore my children.

HECUBA Children, your mother has no city,
No children either. What misery, what sorrow!
Our house now just a wealth of tears.
At least a dead man is immune to grief.   700

CHORUS LEADER Only tears can soothe the afflicted, tears
And dirges sung to the melodies of grief.

ANDROMACHE Mother of the man whose spear cut down
So many Greeks—look at me—do you see this?

HECUBA I see the work of gods who build up towers
Out of nothing, and sweep away like nothing
Towers we think no one could ever topple.

ANDROMACHE My child and I are spoils now being taken
Away, mere loot, nobility in the great turning
Of the wheel become the slaves of others.   710

HECUBA Necessity's a terrifying force. Just now,
Cassandra was taken from me, ripped from my arms.

ANDROMACHE A second Ajax for a second time,
It seems, is threatening your daughter. And yet
More suffering lies in wait for you.

HECUBA I know, there's no end to my suffering.
Evil elbows evil all around me.

ANDROMACHE Polyxena's dead—killed on Achilles' grave,
A final gift to him, a corpse to a corpse.

HECUBA Ah! That pain cuts deeper. So that's what he meant,   720
Talthybius. His riddling words have all come clear.

ANDROMACHE I was there. I saw her myself. I climbed down from the cart
And covered her body with robes and wailed and beat my
        breast.

HECUBA My child, O my poor child, to be sacrificed
So brutally, your throat slit at a dead man's tomb!

ANDROMACHE What was, was. She's dead. But being dead
She's better off than I am, still alive.

HECUBA No, child, you're wrong. They're not the same.
Life means hope, death is nothing at all.

ANDROMACHE Mother, listen, let me reason with you   730
A little, at least enough to ease your mind.
To me, there is no difference between death
And never being born, and death is better
By far than living a life flooded with pain,
Since death ends every suffering. But a man
Who falls from good luck into bad luck suffers
Doubly: from the fall and from remembering
The good luck that he's lost. Polyxena's dead.
But it's as if she never lived at all
For all she knows of what she once went through.   740
I set my sights high for the highest honor,
But, having hit the target, I fell short
Of the happiness I thought I'd won by working
Hard in Hector's house, doing whatever
Custom says a woman ought to do.
Whether or not all women should be blamed
For this, I pushed away that scandalous desire
To be out and about. I kept inside and made sure
My house stayed clear of the gossip that passes for cleverness
Among women. My mind was my only teacher,   750
And content to follow its lead, I held my tongue,
Deferring to my husband when he spoke,

53

Turning to him with a tranquil countenance.
And I knew where and when to have my way,
When I should yield. And yet the reputation
I worked so hard to earn was the very means
Of my destruction, for my good name reached
The Greek camp, and Achilles' son, no less,
Chose me as his wife when I was captured. Now
I'll be a slave in the house of killers of my kin.   760
So tell me, what do I do? If I erase
The memory of my beloved Hector
And give my heart to my new husband, I'll
Betray the dead. But if I don't submit,
He'll hate me; I'll be hated by my master.
I know it's said one night in a man's bed
Is enough to turn a woman's hate to love.
But I despise the woman who casts away
Old love and loves again so easily.
Even a young mare taken from her stable-   770
Mate will buck and whinny when you yoke her,
And yet a horse is just an animal,
A dumb, unreasoning beast, so far below
Us on the scale of nature.
                              But you, my Hector,
My beloved Hector, you were everything
I ever wanted in a husband—strong
In intellect, unsurpassed in wealth, rank, courage.
My first and only love, you took me, still
A virgin, from my father's house. And now
You're dead, and I am being taken far   780
Away to Greece, a prisoner in a ship's hold,
Just a slave.
                 Can't you see, Hecuba,
That Polyxena's death, which makes you weep,
Doesn't compare with what I have to suffer?
Even slim hope, last refuge of all others,
Is denied me. No, I can't fool myself—
However pleasant it would be to do so—
That I'll ever be happy in this world again.

CHORUS LEADER You suffer what I suffer. Telling your troubles,
You teach me to know my own, how deep they are.   790

HECUBA   I've never in my life set foot on a ship,
           But I've seen paintings, and heard people talk,
           So I know that when the wind is soft and steady
           The sailors are all eager to embark,
           One ready at the helm, one at the sails,
           And one to scoop the seeping bilge; but when
           The sea heaves its rough weight across the deck,
           They scurry from their posts and the ship goes
           Where the waves toss it.
                                  So it is with me:
           Troubles swell on gathering trouble so fast,   800
           So deep, I can't describe them. I can't speak,
           Words fail me in the onrush of the waves
           The gods keep sending.
                                  But child, my child, what good
           Can mourning Hector do him now? Your tears
           Won't bring him back. Bow down to your new master.
           By your behavior, lure him into love.
           This way, you'll help us all, you'll please us all,
           You'll see my grandson safely into manhood,
           And maybe his descendants will come home
           To Troy and bring the city back to life.   810

           But now what? Do you see him coming toward us,
           The Greek lackey? To announce some new
           Twist, yet another loathsome new directive?

                         TALTHYBIUS *enters with armed attendants.*

TALTHYBIUS Wife of Hector, once the bravest man
            In Troy, don't hate me for what I've come to tell you.
            Against my will, I must announce the common
            Will of the Greeks and of Pelops's noble grandsons.
            I'd rather tell you anything but this.

ANDROMACHE What does "this" mean? You're hinting at something
                    hateful.

TALTHYBIUS It's been decided that your son—ah, how can I say
                    this?   820

ANDROMACHE   Surely you're not—you can't mean we'll have different
                            masters?

TALTHYBIUS   No Greek will ever own him. No, I don't mean that.

ANDROMACHE   Will he be left here? Last of the Trojan race?

TALTHYBIUS   No—but there's no easy way to tell the bad news.

ANDROMACHE   Thanks for your courtesy—unless the news is awful.

TALTHYBIUS   They're going to kill your boy. That's the sorry truth. Now
                            you know.

ANDROMACHE   You can't... this isn't... it's too cruel to be believed.

TALTHYBIUS   Odysseus's proposal won in the Greek assembly...

ANDROMACHE   *AIAI*, no one could bear this, grief beyond grief.

TALTHYBIUS   ...not to let a hero's son survive.   830

ANDROMACHE   May his own son win treatment just as kind.

TALTHYBIUS   He said your boy's to be flung from the Trojan walls.
                     But don't resist, it will be wiser not to.
                     Let your son go now, don't cling to him, don't fight this—
                     Grieve nobly, befitting your nobility,
                     And don't pretend you're strong. You have no power,
                     And no one's rushing to defend you. Look
                     Where you are, what you have come to—your city
                     Ruined, your husband dead. You're beaten down.
                     We're capable of doing whatever we want with you,   840
                     Just one woman. Don't struggle anymore,
                     Don't provoke us, or make things worse for you
                     By cursing us, for if you make us angry,
                     The army might decide to show this son
                     Of yours no mercy, leaving his corpse unburied.
                     Hush now, shoulder your troubles as you should;
                     You will not leave your dead child without his rite
                     Of burial, and the Greeks will be less cruel.

ANDROMACHE O my sweet child, too loved, too doted on,
                    Now you will be killed by enemies, leaving   850
                    Your mother bereft. What ought to have been your
                          haven,
                    Your father's high birth, only brings you death,
                    His courage your undoing. When I came
                    To Hector's house, I never thought those vows,
                    That marriage bed, would lead to misery.
                    I thought I had given birth to a king over all
                    Of fertile Asia's wealth. I never thought
                    I bore you to be slaughtered by the Greeks.
                    Is that why you cry, too, child? Do you see
                    What's soon to happen, what they're about to do?   860
                    Why hold tight to me, clinging to my dress
                    Like a young bird burrowing for safety
                    Under my wings? No one can save you; Hector
                    Can't rise from his grave, his famous spear in hand,
                    Nor any of his kin, nor any strong-armed
                    Soldier from the Trojan ranks. No one will come
                    To stop them or even pity you when they hurl you
                    From that great height, and your thin neck shatters,
                    Snuffing your life out. O my little one,
                    So precious to your mother, O the unbearable   870
                    Sweet scent of your skin! So it was all for nothing
                    That I suckled you at this breast and swaddled you
                    And fussed and worried, wearing myself out.
                    Now kiss your mother one last time, come hug her
                    Who gave you life, one final time your arms
                    Around my neck, your lips on mine. O Greeks,

                    Not even a barbarian could invent
                    Atrocities like this—why kill this child,
                    What has he done to you? Whom has he ever harmed?
                    Helen, daughter of Tyndareus's house,   880
                    Zeus was never your father—I'll tell you who
                    Your many fathers were: Vengeance, Envy,
                    Murder, Death, and all the Pestilence
                    The earth can breed! Zeus never gave you birth,
                    You plague both to barbarians and Greeks.
                    Die! Die, you whose shining eyes
                    Brought such dark and ugly dying to
                    The famous plains of Troy.
                                          But go on, take him,

Carry him off, hurl him to his destruction,
Or even eat his flesh, if that's your will.   890
The gods are surely murdering a mother
Who cannot save her child from death.
                                        So throw
Some rag around my wretched body and hurl me
Into the ship's hold. My own child's blood
Is paving the road I take to this new marriage.

> TALTHYBIUS *takes the child from the cart, which leaves the*
> *stage carrying* ANDROMACHE *away.*

CHORUS LEADER Unhappy Troy, no one could count the thousands
Upon thousands of your children who've been slaughtered
For the sake of one woman and her evil marriage!

TALTHYBIUS Let's go, child, come along now: held no longer
Within your heartsick mother's loving arms,   900
You must go to the highest rampart of the ancient wall
Where it's been ordered you will meet your end.
(to the guards) Take him.
                                The man who bears an order cruel
As this ought to be all ruthlessness,
Someone with a heart more shameless than mine.
As it is, my heart just isn't hard enough.

> TALTHYBIUS *exits in the direction of the Greek camp. The*
> *guards carry* ASTYANAX *away in the opposite direction.*

HECUBA O child, child of my own sad child, your life
Is being ripped from us, your mother and I.
What now? What next? What can I do to help you
From this harsh fate? I can beat my head and breast,   910
That much I can do, I have that much power.
O child, O city—what's left to suffer? How much further
Can we fall into complete destruction?

CHORUS Telamon, King of Salamis,   *Strophe 1*
Rich haunt of bees, the wave-loud island you settled,
Island that faces the steep slope sacred to Athena
From which she brought forth
The first branch of the gray-green olive,

Crown and bright splendor to shining Athens,
Telamon, you boldly came with Alcmena's son,   920
The archer, to raze Troy,
This city that was ours
Only a little while ago.

Cheated of the horses he had won,   *Antistrophe 1*
Heracles led out of Greece the flower of its
      might,
Sea oars easing where the Simois flows; and after
      making fast
The ships' stern-cables he brought forth
His faultless bow, brought death to Laomedon
As the fiery red gale roared up and over the chiseled
Stonework of Apollo, sweeping through Troy.   930
Twice in two pummeling storms,
The red spear leveled Dardanians
All around the walls.

Useless son   *Strophe 2*
Of Laomedon,
Glorious servant boy,
You prance
Among the golden wine jugs,
Filling the cups of Zeus,
Looking or not   940
Looking down
Upon your native city
As it burns to nothing,
While like a mother bird
Crying for its chicks,
The beach cries
Everywhere
Along its length,
Crying out
For husbands here,   950
And there for children,
For palsied mothers, too,
The beach cries, and it is
All gone, your dew-bright
Bathing places,

The tracks you ran on,
Gone, and yet beside
The luminous throne
Of Zeus your face
Is no less charming   960
In its freshness,
Utterly serene.
The Greek spear has effaced the land of Priam.

And Love,   *Antistrophe 2*
Once so at home
In the great halls of Dardanus,
Love deep rooted
In the sky-born minds,
How high, how
Lofty you built   970
Up Troy once,
Marrying her to the gods!
But what good does it do now,
Blaming Zeus for that?
Dawn, friend to mortals,
Rising on white wings
Of light, looked on
As the land burned,
As Pergamum was razed,
Though she herself   980
Married a man from here,
This country, the father
Of her children came
From this country, a man who
Then was lifted
In the four-horse
Golden chariot to the stars
Where we believed
His shining meant
Eternal promise   990
For our homeland.
But the gods
Who loved Troy once love Troy no longer.

MENELAUS *enters with armed attendants.*

MENELAUS   How gloriously bright the sun is shining
            On this longed-for day when I finally get to lay
            My two hands on that woman, my wife. And yet
            I came to Troy, not as most people think,
            For her alone, or her primarily,
            But to exact revenge against the man—
            A guest I honored in my very home—   1000
            Who then betrayed me, stealing my wife away.
            Well, he's gotten his just deserts, I can tell you that;
            Thanks to the gods, the Greek spear was the last thing
            He and his homeland felt before they fell.
            But now that's over with, and here I am
            For her, the Spartan (I can't even bring myself
            To say her name, though I was married to her once).
            She's just another Trojan woman, a prisoner
            Among prisoners, a slave, and those who fought
            On my behalf have given her back to me   1010
            To kill or bring home alive to Argos,
            If that's what I want to do. I have decided
            Not to bother myself with Helen's death
            Here, but to sail back to Greece with her
            And kill her there in punishment for all
            The friends who fell beside me on the plains of Troy.
            (to the guards) Men, go inside and get her, bring her out,
            Drag her by the hair so many died for.
            When the wind is right, we'll take her home to Greece.

HECUBA   O you who somehow cup the whole earth   1020
            Yet have your seat upon it, you boundless mystery
            Called Zeus, whether you are the fixed law of Nature
            Or man's Mind—whoever you are, I invoke you;
            For walking your own way in silence you guide
                    the tangled
            Affairs of men toward the path of Justice.

MENELAUS   A strange way to pray to the gods, if it's even a prayer.

HECUBA   You're right to want to kill your wife, Menelaus.
            But whatever you do, don't look at her, don't
            Look at her eyes: they ambush with desire,
            They snare the eyes of men, and as for her,   1030
            She's hell for cities, burning hell for homes.

Her power will trick you into helplessness.
You and I, we've suffered from her charm,
The way so many others have. We know.

> HELEN *is led on stage by* MENELAUS's *men. She is not dressed*
> *in mourning like the other women, but is elegantly dressed*
> *and with hair unshorn, and she resists her guards with*
> *gestures of haughty disdain.*

HELEN   Menelaus, how could you treat me like this
Just when we're reunited? How could you let
Your flunkies put their filthy hands on me
And drag me here? You must really hate me.
Yet all the same, I want to ask you something:
Have the Greeks decided if I'll live or die?   1040

MENELAUS   No, not precisely. But the army did
Turn you over to me, expecting I
Would kill you, since I am the one you betrayed.

HELEN   May I respond to that? May I try to show you
That it would be unjust if you did kill me?

MENELAUS   I came here to see you die, not to hear you speak.

HECUBA   Let her speak, Menelaus. She shouldn't die
Without a hearing. But let me be the one
To cross-examine her. I know better than you
How she has made Troy suffer. A free   1050
Debate will kill her. She'll have no escape.

MENELAUS   This will take time. But if she wants to talk,
She may do so. Make no mistake, though,
I'm granting her this opportunity
Because of you, for your sake, not for hers.

HELEN   You hate me so much that maybe you won't listen
To anything I say, no matter how well I say it.
Nevertheless, I know exactly what
You would accuse me of, if you did speak,
And I have arguments to make in my defense.   1060
First, Paris was the cause of all our trouble.

This woman here gave birth to Paris, so she's
The mother of the cause of all our trouble.
Secondly, her husband, the old king,
Led to Troy's downfall and mine by letting him live,
The infant, Alexander, as he was called then,
The murderous firebrand Hecuba dreamed of.
Think about what happened after that.
Paris judged a contest of three goddesses:
Pallas Athena offered him glory in battle,   1070
Leading the Trojan army to victory over Greece.
Hera promised he'd rule over Asia,
And all of Europe, if the contest went her way.
And struck with wonder at my incomparable
Appearance, Aphrodite promised me
To him if he would say she far surpassed
The other goddesses in beauty. Consider
What followed from that: Aphrodite won.
I married Paris, and Greece reaped the benefit.
No barbarians have taken you in thrall,   1080
Either through warfare or the tyrant's lash,
And yet what's given Greece such great good luck
Has only meant bad luck for me. Once brokered
For my beauty, I'm hated by the very ones
Who ought to crown my head in gratitude.

I know you'll say I haven't yet addressed
The major charge against me: my alleged elopement.
I did escape in secret from your house.
I admit that. But listen, when Paris, or Alexander,
Or Hecuba's vengeful bane, whatever you want   1090
To call him, when he came here, Aphrodite,
No meager goddess, was right there by his side.
And this was the man you left me alone with, you fool,
In your own house when you sailed off to Crete.
But I must ask myself, not you, about
What happened next. What was I thinking when
I followed him, that stranger, from my home,
Betraying home and country? Blame the goddess
For this, not me—go punish her if you think
You're mightier than Zeus, who lords it over   1100
All the other gods but is himself
A slave to her. No, I should be forgiven.

Oh, I can just see what you're thinking now,
The empty argument you'll bring against me:
Once Paris was dead and buried, and the god-
Made marriage was dissolved, why didn't I leave
His house and return to the Argive ships?
In fact, I did. I kept trying to leave—
The tower guards will tell you, for they saw me,
And the watchmen from the walls, they saw me too,   1110
And often caught me as I tried to let
Myself down from the battlements by rope.
How then, dear husband, would it be just to kill me?
Paris took me by force, I was more slave
Than bride. What have I won but slavery?
This was all the gods' fault. Your desire
To overrule them is dangerously stupid.

CHORUS My queen, protect your children and your homeland
        From the insidious bewitchment of her words—
        It's terrible how well the guilty one can speak.   1120

HECUBA First, I'll defend the goddesses against
        This woman's libelous attack. Would Hera
        Or the virgin goddess Pallas Athena ever
        Be so incredibly foolish as to either
        Sell out Argos to the barbarians
        Or let Athenians become the slaves of Troy?
        I don't believe it for a second. I don't
        Believe the goddesses would come to Ida
        For games, much less for a silly Miss Olympus
        Competition. Why would Hera even   1130
        Be concerned with being beautiful?
        So she can snare a husband better than Zeus?
        Is Athena now on the lookout for a spouse,
        Despite her having asked her father once
        To let her stay a virgin, because she hated marriage?
        Don't gloss over your own bad actions
        By making the gods out to be fools. You won't
        Persuade anyone with any common sense.
        You claim that Aphrodite accompanied
        My son to Menelaus's house, which is   1140
        Such a laughable idea, since she's
        A god and could have stayed right where she was

64

In heaven and still transported you and all
Of Amyclae as well to Troy, if she desired.
Let's face it: my son was the handsomest of men.
You saw him, and instantly your mind itself
Turned into Aphrodite, who after all
Is just the name we give to lust run wild.
It's no coincidence that "witless" rhymes
With Cypris. Yes, you saw my son dressed up   1150
In Asian splendor, his gold all glittering,
And you fell hard for him; he made you crazy.
He made you chafe against your austere life
In Argos, and dream of getting free of Sparta
So the flash flood of your opulent appetites
Could level the rich city of Troy. Menelaus's palace
Was too small; it cramped your riotous desires.
Well then: you say that my son dragged you off
By force. If that is so, what Spartan woman
Saw you? Did you cry out? Your young twin brothers,   1160
Castor and Pollux, weren't they still at home,
Not yet ascended to the stars? Why didn't they help you?

And don't forget how you behaved in Troy.
When the Greeks tracked you down, and the bloody war
Had started, your heart turned with the tide of battle:
When the Greeks got the upper hand, you'd taunt
My son by praising Menelaus, saying
What a glorious warrior he was,
What a superior lover, but when the Trojans
Did well, it was as if you didn't know   1170
Who Menelaus was. In other words,
You had no loyalty to anyone,
But followed fortune, drifting where it went.
You claim that you attempted to escape,
That you would secretly shinny down
The walls by rope, and that we kept you here
Against your will. So why did no one ever
Find you with a noose around your neck,
Or sharpening a sword that you could fall on,
The kind of deed a noble woman heartsick   1180
For her absent husband would have surely done?
The fact is time and time again I told you,
"Leave us, my daughter, there are other girls
My sons can marry. I'll help you sneak away,

I'll take you secretly to the Achaean ships.
Please end this war between the Greeks and Trojans."
You spurned me, spurned my advice. Your need
For adoration overran the palace,
We—to your eyes all barbarians—couldn't
Bow down enough before you. That's all you wanted.   1190
And after all of this you have the nerve,
You monster, you brazen witch, to come out here
Tricked out in all your finery, to breathe
The same air your husband breathes. It would
          have been
More fitting had you appeared in filthy rags,
Your head shaved, trembling, humbled by fear.
Given your many crimes, you should be drowned
In shame, not basking in arrogance.
                                                  Menelaus,
I'm finished speaking. You've heard my argument.
Now crown your country's honor with a deed   1200
Worthy of your own, and kill this woman.
You'll make her an example to all other wives:
That anyone who betrays her husband dies.

CHORUS   Menelaus, do what the honor of your house
          And all your ancestors demands, and give
          Your wife the justice she deserves. You'll scour
          From Greece the stain of what she's done
          And thus earn even your enemy's respect.

MENELAUS   I'm completely on your side in this debate.
           This woman freely exchanged my home for a
                     stranger's,   1210
           My bed for his. She invokes Aphrodite
           As a smoke screen.
                     (to HELEN) So go you, go find the people
           Who'll kill you by stoning, who'll see to it that you pay
           In one instant for all the Greeks' long labors,
           Revenge at last for all the Greeks have suffered.
           Dying, you'll learn not to shame and dishonor me.

HELEN   No! I'm on my knees. The gods sent these evils.
          I don't deserve to die. Forgive me, please!

HECUBA   Keep faith with all the comrades she has killed.
          I beg you for their sake, and for their children.   1220

MENELAUS Be quiet, Hecuba. I haven't listened
          To a word she's said. I'm ordering my men
          To take her to the ships for the journey home.

HECUBA   But don't let her sail on the same ship with you.

MENELAUS Why not? Has she gained weight? Is she too
                  heavy now?

HECUBA   When a lover falls hard, he falls for good.

MENELAUS That depends on how the beloved behaves.
          Still, what you suggest makes sense, and I agree
          That she should travel on another ship.
          And when we get to Argos, she will die   1230
          The wretched death a slut like her deserves.
          I'll make her an example to all women
          To be faithful. No easy thing to do, I know,
          But her death will check their foolishness with fear,
          Even the ones more shameless than herself.

                  MENELAUS *departs, followed by his attendants, with* HELEN
                                                          in tow.

CHORUS   So, Zeus—so this was your desire?   *Strophe 1*
          To betray us all to the Achaeans;
          To betray your Trojan temple
          And its altar gauzed with incense
          And myrrh in sweet clouds   1240
          Rising to the heavens;
          To betray sacred Pergamum
          And the ivy-darkened draws,
          The valleys of Mount Ida,
          Their rivers bright with snowmelt
          And the extravagant
          Sweep of sky to the far horizon
          Cut by the dawn's first ray,
          This place so luminous and holy.

Gone—all your sacrifices; gone—   *Antistrophe 1*   1250
The joyful singing of your choirs
In the dark-enveloped,
Night-long festivals we made
To celebrate our gods;
Gone—the hammered gold
Figures and the sacrificial
Moon cakes, twelve in all.
I have to wonder, Lord,
What you had in mind
As you looked down   1260
From your astral throne
On the collapsing city,
On the waves of flames that crashed
         against it.

O my beloved husband,   *Strophe 2*
Unburied, untouched
By lustral water, now
You'll wander, restless,
While I'll be taken from you
Over seas in a swift ship
Winged by oars to Argos,   1270
Where horses graze,
To the sky-touched walls
The Cyclopes built.
And the children crowd
To the gates, they press
Against the gates,
And cling, and call out
"Help me, mother, help me!"
They call out, crying,
"Don't let   1280
The Greeks take me
Away from you,
All by myself
To the ship's black hull;
Don't let them
Take me to Salamis
With its holy temples,
Or to the high peak
Of the Isthmus

Between two seas,   1290
Where Pelops set his palace gates."

May Zeus himself hurl down   *Antistrophe 2*
Aegean lightning bolts
Against the ship that carries
Menelaus over the sea;
May the god-flung fire
Split his ship in two,
So that one row of oars
Falls burning from the other.
May they all suffer   1300
For sending me in tears
From Troy, far from my homeland,
To slave my life away
In Greece while that one,
Zeus's daughter, holds
In her hand the golden
Mirror girls love to gaze into.
May Menelaus never reach
His home in Sparta, never
Warm himself again   1310
At his ancestral hearth;
May he never reach
The precincts of Pitane,
The bronze gate of Athena's temple,
Now that he's got back
The shame of Greece,
Whose outrageous marriage
Brought devastation
Here to the shores of Simois.

TALTHYBIUS *returns, with men carrying the body of* ASTYANAX
laid on Hector's shield.

CHORUS Oh no!   1320
        A new disaster in the wake
        Of wave after
        Wave of new disaster.
        Sad women of Troy,
        Here is the murdered body

Of Astyanax, hurled
Like a discus from the walls.

TALTHYBIUS   Hecuba, only one ship remains. The oars
Are poised above the salt spray, ready to take back
To Phthia what's left of the spoils of Achilles' son.   1330
Neoptolemus himself has set sail already.
He heard bad news concerning Peleus:
Acastus, Pelias's son, has banished him.
That's why Neoptolemus vanished in such a hurry
And took Andromache with him. It made me weep
To hear her crying as she left, to hear her
Grieving out loud for her homeland, saying
Goodbye one final time to Hector's tomb,
And begging Neoptolemus to bury
Astyanax's body, your own son's son   1340
Flung to his cruel death from the city walls.
She pleaded with Neoptolemus not to take
This shield—the bronze-backed shield that terrified
The Greeks when Hector wore it across his body
As Troy's defender—to Peleus's house, into the very
Bedroom where she'd become Neoptolemus's bride.
She begged him to leave it here, for the child's
Burial, not in a cedar coffin and a tomb,
Hewn of stone, but on the shield itself.
She begged him to give the child into your care,   1350
Give him to you, so you could swaddle him
In winding sheets and garlands, adorning him
As best you can with what little you have left.
You see, it's up to you to do this now
Because she's gone, because her master's haste
Prevented her from burying the child herself.
Now listen: when you've got the body ready,
We'll bury it and set sail. So do what you've
       been told
To do as quickly as you can. I've spared
You one chore, though. As we crossed over
       the waters   1360
Of the Scamander, I washed the little corpse
And cleaned its wounds. And now I'll even break
The ground and dig his grave so that together

You and I can get these last chores done
And set the ship firm on the path for home.

TALTHYBIUS *and part of his escort exit, leaving two soldiers still
holding the shield with* ASTYANAX's *body laid out upon it.*

HECUBA Set down Hector's round shield on the ground.
Oh, how I suffer at the hateful sight of it.
You Greeks, your weaponry holds more strength
        than wisdom.
Why kill this child? Why slaughter him in such
A new and brutal way? What were you scared of?   1370
That he might one day make Troy rise again?
If so, your vaunted strength amounts to nothing.
For even when Hector was at his peak in battle,
With thousands of comrades fighting by his side,
We still fell, all of us, one by one, and now,
Now that the city's gone, and we're all destroyed,
You're still afraid of him, this little child.
I loathe this fear no reason penetrates.

(turning to the body of ASTYANAX*)*

And you, beloved child, how miserably you've died.
If you had grown to manhood, and had married,   1380
And come into possession of a kingdom
Godlike in power, and only then had died,
Defending the city, we could have said you'd lived
A happy life, that is, if happiness
Resides in things like that. But no; however
Much you may have been aware of what
Your heritage would be, you never lived
To know it, you never lived to make it yours.
Instead, your father's walls, the battlements
Apollo built, have ripped the curls from your head,   1390
The curls your mother fussed over and kissed,
The skull now broken, bright blood gushing out
Like wicked laughter between the bones. I won't
Conceal or soften the brutality of this.
Your hands so sweetly like your father's
Hang broken at the joints. Look at them. Look

At the sweet lips that made great promises
To me—promises they couldn't keep, child—
As you stood clinging to my dress and said,
"Grandmother, I'll cut you my thickest lock of hair   1400
When you die and bring my best friends to
          your tomb
And say goodbye to you with all my heart."
But it is I who say goodbye to you,
Who bury you, poor boy, and you so young
And I so old, an old heartbroken woman,
Without a child, without a city. O god,
What were they for, all those embraces, all
The daily, nightly coddling of you?
They've come to nothing. What kind of epitaph
Would any poet write upon your tomb: 1410
"The Greeks were terrified of this little boy,
And so they killed him." What a shameful
          indictment
Of Greece that epitaph would be.
                              No, child, no,
You haven't won your father's heritage,
But you'll possess, if only as a coffin,
His bronze-backed shield.
                              O shield, that Hector held,
That guarded his thick arm, he cared for you
So well and yet you lost him. And all that's left
Is the sweet indentation of his body
On your sling, the sweat stain on your
          well-worked rim,   1420
The sweat, which in the heat of battle dripped
From Hector's face, his chin pressed hard
          against you.

          (turning to her attendants, who enter the central hut)

Come now, time to adorn the wretched body,
As much as we can, given our circumstances.
Fate won't permit us to do a lot for him.
But what we have he'll get.
                              That man who feels
Safe in his blessings and rejoices is
A fool. The way of fortune is to leap

About in all directions like a wild man,
And no one controls his happiness for long. 1430

HECUBA's *attendants bring a fine robe and other adornments*
for the child's body.

CHORUS Here are your women who bring from the
      Trojan spoils
What little remains to adorn the body with.

HECUBA My child, I lay upon you what precious things
We still have left from what had once been yours,
Adorning you with them but not in joy,
No, not for any victory you might
Have won over your peers with horse or bow,
Contests we honor to sate the need for strife.
No, this is all that Helen left us, all
She didn't steal, god-hated as she is, 1440
Who robbed us blind and then destroyed your life
And sent our whole house, all of it, down to ruin.

CHORUS Ah, how
You break my heart, how you break
My heart so deeply, you
Who were once a great prince in my city.

HECUBA The dazzling splendor of these Phrygian robes
That I lay upon you now should have adorned you
At your marriage to some great Asian princess.
O dearest shield of Hector, you who were 1450
Supreme in victory, mother of conquests
Too many to count, cradle this little crown
I place upon you, you no more alive than he is,
No more alive yet deathless in your way,
More honorable by far than any weapon
Of Odysseus, that cunning liar.

CHORUS *AIAI, AIAI.* The earth has opened for you, child,
Our unbearable grief.
Cry out, dear mother . . .

HECUBA *AIAI.* 1460

CHORUS   . . . a dirge for the dead.

HECUBA   O god!

CHORUS   O god, for the sufferings that will not be forgotten!

HECUBA   I can cover your wounds with bandages,
         A doctor come too late, his skills now useless.
         Your father will care for you among the dead.

CHORUS   Beat your head, your face,
         Beat it over and over
         The way the oar stroke beats the water.

HECUBA   Dear women . . .   1470

CHORUS   Hecuba, cry out whatever is in your mind.

HECUBA   So in the end the gods did nothing for us.
         Anguish and more anguish is all they ever brought,
         And above all hatred for my city. And all
         Our sacrifices counted for nothing. And yet
         If god's fist hadn't battered us to nothing,
         What fame would we have had? We would have lived
         Unsung, unknown in song by those to come.
         Go bury the corpse now in its paltry tomb.
         It has what flowers it needs. And anyway   1480
         What difference can a flowery display
         Make to the one who's dead? Adornments like these
         Are only the cheap solace of the living.

                          Attendants carry off the child's body.

CHORUS   *IO, IO.*
         Saddest of all mothers,
         All your fine hopes
         Have been mangled and torn
         Apart inside you.
                          High birth,
         Vast wealth—child, you
         Nonetheless   1490
         Died miserably.

74

But look now, up there!
Men on Ilium's high walls,
Swinging torches whose flames
Gather and swell in bright waves,
Like burning water.
This can only mean
More misery for Troy.

TALTHYBIUS *returns with an escort.*

TALTHYBIUS I call out to the captains who've been ordered
To set fire to Priam's city—don't let the flame   1500
Rest easy in your hand but hurl the fire now,
And as soon as Ilium's citadel crumbles and falls,
We'll gladly, at last, sail home from Troy.
                                        And you,
You daughters of the Trojans, I want my single order
To do the work of two, so when the captains
Sound the echoing trumpet blare, start moving
To the ships that wait to take you from this land.
And you go too, saddest of all old women.
Odysseus has sent these men for you, whose lot
Drives you from your homeland to be his slave.   1510

HECUBA Ah, how miserable I am! This, this
Is the final destination of all my suffering,
Where all of it was heading all along.
I'm leaving my country; my city's sunk in flame.
Come, old feet, hobble as best you can,
So one last time I can salute the city
In all its misery. O Troy, whose greatness
Roared like a wind across all Asian lands,
Your very name is being disappeared,
The last thing stolen. They're burning you to nothing.   1520
And we are dragged away, already slaves.
O gods! O gods! Yet why invoke them now?
When did they ever listen to my cries?
Let's run into the pyre. Better to die
Here burning in my homeland as it burns.

HECUBA *staggers toward the walls, but is stopped by Odysseus's*
                                                        men.

TALTHYBIUS   Poor woman, your mind has broken under the weight
Of all your pain. Men, lead her off, no shirking!
Bring her to Odysseus, her owner.

HECUBA   *OTOTOTOI.*   *Strophe 1*
Zeus, son of Cronus, lord of Phrygia,   1530
Founding father, do you see what's happening,
How we suffer, the disgrace
To the Dardanian line?

CHORUS   He has seen, he sees, and yet
The great city
Is a city no more. There is no Troy.

HECUBA   *OTOTOTOI.*   *Antistrophe 1*
Ilium blazes. Flames break in waves
Over the houses of Pergamum,
Against the citadel, along   1540
The summit of the walls.

CHORUS   Our homeland fallen to the spear
Is dwindling, as smoke
Thins to nothing on a wing of wind,

HECUBA   O land where all my children flourished.   *Strophe 2*

CHORUS   Alas!

HECUBA   O children
Hear me, hear
Your mother's cry.

CHORUS   You're crying to the dead,   1550
Singing the saddest dirge.

HECUBA *falls to the ground.*

HECUBA   My old body sinks to the ground
And I beat the earth with both hands.

CHORUS   I follow you and kneel
To earth, calling

My poor husband
In the world beneath.

HECUBA   We're led away, dragged...

CHORUS   Pain cries through you, only pain.

HECUBA   .... to a slave's house.   1560

CHORUS   ... and far from my country, too.

HECUBA   O Priam, Priam, unburied,
Lonely in death,
You can't know
How they're destroying me.

CHORUS   Black Death, Death holy
Amid unholy butchery
Has closed his eyes.

HECUBA   O temples of the gods, beloved city...   *Antistrophe 2*

CHORUS   Alas!   1570

HECUBA   ... the murdering flame
And the spear's strength
Own you now.

CHORUS   You'll fall to the cherished earth,
Straight into namelessness.

HECUBA   And black wings of ash
And smoke now open wide
To hide the city from my sight.

CHORUS   The very name of the land
Will be lost soon.   1580
All we've known is vanishing,
Troy is no longer Troy.

HECUBA   Did you hear that,
Did you feel it?

CHORUS Yes, the towers crashing.

HECUBA The earth split open...

CHORUS ...to swallow up the city.

                                        HECUBA *rises one last time.*

HECUBA *IO, IO.* Time to go, you trembling
        Unsteady limbs, go forward now
        Into the day of slavery.   1590

CHORUS Grieve for the saddest of all cities.
        But as you grieve
        Keep moving to the Achaean ships.

                        All exit in the direction of the ships.

NOTES ON THE TEXT

Note on the scene The arrangement proposed in this translation is hypothetical. It is possible that all the entrances of the Trojan women were made from the central door of the scene building, but far less likely that they entered from the side entrances—with the exception of Andromache, who comes on in a cart from the direction of the city, and presumably Helen, who is clearly accorded special treatment and presumably also enters from the same side, since the other side will be used for movements to and from the Greek camp. In our reconstruction, tents (cf. **196/** 176) are visible on either side of the stage, from which the women of the chorus emerge in two groups. The central door is reserved for Trojan royals, and from it emerge only Hecuba, before the beginning of the prologue, and Cassandra. Greeks enter from the camp by one of the side entrances; the other is used for the entrances of Andromache and Helen, the departure of Astyanax, and the return of his corpse.

1–171 / 1–152 *Prologue* The prologue (construed according to the definition in Aristotle's *Poetics* 52b19 as everything that comes before the entry of the chorus) is formally typical for Euripides: a spoken monologue followed by dialogue, setting out the requisite background, followed by a lyric monody of one of the main characters. Within that frame, however, it is in many ways extraordinary. Two things deserve special notice: first, the gods who introduce the play go far beyond its background, and even its plot, by predicting more distant consequences of the action we are about to see. The divine retribution foretold for the Greeks who have sacked Troy extends the horizons of the drama in time and opens up the meaning of the action to a broader "gods' eye" view of its meaning. Secondly, lines **43–5** /36–8 reveal that their entrance has been preceded by the arrival and collapse of Hecuba, whose suffering is thus an immediate part of the audience's experience of the divine dialogue. (For the staging of this scene, see the Introduction, p. 12.)

1 / 1 *I am Poseidon* Elsewhere in the surviving plays of Euripides, speeches by gods also open *Alcestis, Hippolytus, Ion,* and *Bacchae.* In *Alcestis,* the opening monologue is also followed by dialogue with another divinity.

5–6 / 5 *Phoebus Apollo / And I* According to legend, the gods were obliged to hire themselves out to King Laomedon for a year, during which they did the building of Troy's walls. (These are the walls destroyed by Heracles; see **924–30/809–16** with note on **924–5**.)

9 / 10 *Pallas Athena willed* Literally, "by the designs of Pallas Athena," who is depicted, in line with her portrayal by Homer, as the great friend of the Greeks and enemy of the Trojan cause. Poseidon, who is also presented in the *Iliad* as pro-Greek, here becomes a friend of Troy (see **7/6–7, 28–9/23–5**), no doubt in part to give a more sympathetic tone to the account of the city's fall, but also to make the agreement of the gods to spoil the Greek triumph an act agreed to both by friend and foe alike, and indeed a source of reconciliation between them (cf. **58–84/ 48–74**).

15 / 15 *The sacred groves are now deserted* "Deserted" or "desolate" (Greek *erêmos*) is often repeated to describe the fate of Troy. See **30/26, 107/97** (with note), **653/564,** and **697/603** (with note).

15–6 / 15–6 *blood / Oozes from the temples of the gods* The sacrilege attendant upon the Greeks' sack of Troy is an emphatic theme of the prologue. Priam has been slain at the altar of Zeus (**17–8/16–7**); Cassandra, Apollo's virgin, who has been dragged from Athena's temple by force (**80/70**), will be made to serve as Agamemnon's concubine (**50–3/41–4**); temples and graves have been desecrated (**105–8/95–7**).

18 / 17 *Zeus, protector of the hearth* Zeus in his aspect as protector of the family. Altars to Zeus *Herkeios* stood within the household enclosure, and suppliants could take refuge there. There is a particular irony here, because Priam, Troy's patriarch, was murdered by Achilles' son, Neoptolemus, at the very altar that should have provided safety. This version is attested in the Epic Cycle and finds detailed and memorable expression in Virgil's *Aeneid* 2.526–58. Cf. Hecuba's lament for her husband's death at **562–4/ 481–3**.

26 / 24 *Hera the Argive goddess* The epithet, appropriate to Hera's role as partisan of the Greeks, comes from her most famous sanctuary, the Argive Heraion. The most obvious reason for the partisanship of Hera and Athena, not stated here, will be suggested by Helen's account of their loss of the "beauty contest" to Aphrodite, **1069–78/924–33**.

28 / 25 *I'm deserting Troy* Gods abandon cities that fall, just as they leave the presence
of mortals when they die. For the former, cf. Euripides' *Hippolytus*
1437–9, where Artemis departs to avoid witnessing the hero's death; for
the latter, cf. Aeschylus's *Seven Against Thebes* 217–8: "It is said that the
gods of a captured city desert it."

36 / 31 *the sons of Theseus* This might refer to Demophon and Acamas, the sons of
Athens's legendary King Theseus; according to the Epic Cycle and later
mythographers, they played a role in the battle for Troy. Alternatively, it
could simply be a kenning for the Athenians. In any case, Euripides is
making a point of the Athenian presence in this war that is all but
nonexistent in the *Iliad* (merely a reference to an Athenian force
under a certain Menestheus in the Catalogue of Ships, 2.546–54); and
Athens will return as the Trojan women's hoped-for place of captivity
(**231–3**/207–8).

42 / 35 *daughter of Tyndareus* Helen is one of the many figures of legend to whom the
Greeks attributed both a human and a divine (in her case, Zeus) father.
The fact that a deity refers to her mortal father need not suggest
skepticism about the tradition of Zeus's paternity, but it may be con-
sidered part of the disapproval of Helen ("rightly treated as a captive
slave," according to Poseidon) that runs throughout the play. At 880–1/
766, on the other hand, Andromache will use the tradition of Tyndareus
precisely to deny Zeus's paternity.

48 / 41 *Priam . . . is dead. Her sons are dead* The word translated "dead" is *phroudos*,
"gone," "vanished." The word recurs at **993**/859, **1245**/1071, **1334**/1130,
1581/1323, in four of the instances emphatically at the beginning of a line.

80 / 70 *Ajax dragged Cassandra off by force* This is the "lesser" Ajax, son of Oileus,
from Locri; see Glossary.

92 / 82 *your task is the Aegean Sea* Poseidon, as god of the sea, is the appropriate deity
for this assignment, as his response makes clear.

94 / 83 *with towering waves* Literally, "with third waves" (*triskumiais*), which the
Greeks thought were always the highest.

99–101 / 89–90 *Mykonos, / . . . Delos, Skyros, Lemnos, / and the promontories of Caphereus* the islands to be "clogged with countless bodies" cover a broad
swath of the Aegean, suggesting the magnitude of the storm Poseidon
will raise. The cliffs of Caphereus, on the coast of Euboea, is the site
where Nauplios lit a huge fire to attract Greek ships to the treacherous
rocks below, in revenge for the Greeks' killing of his son Palamedes at

Troy (cf. Euripides' *Helen* 1126–310). This may well have been foretold in Euripides' *Palamedes* (see the Introduction, p. 9).

107 / 97 *for all his pillaging* literally, "having given them [temples, etc.] over to desolation [*erêmiai*]"; see note on 15.

109–71 / 98–150 Hecuba's monody is a long, intense expression of grief, beginning (to judge from its meter) with recitative, then moving to full lyric mode at 122/141. Hecuba begins with her own sorrows; turns to song to address their cause, the Greek expedition against her city; and at 138/156 reverts to her own sorrows and those of the other women of Troy, who enter in response to her lament.

114–5 / 102 *Sail / With the hard current of the strait* This is first in a chain of nautical metaphors and images, in which imagined ships express abandonment to the power of fate and the rocking movement of the grieving body (134–5/115–6), and the real vessels of the Greek fleet evoke the arrival of Troy's destroyers (141–9/122–30). The language of ships and the sea is at once a reminder of the disasters that Poseidon has just foretold for the Greeks, and a foreshadowing of the Trojan women's voyage to their slave homes, thoughts of which will dominate the initial choral song, the *parodos*.

139–40 / 120–1 *the song / Of troubles no one dances to* The other leading figure of the monody is music. "Why sing / a dirge?" asks Hecuba (127–8/111), and this is her answer: the song of lament is all that is left to those bereft of everything they value. Music returns in the guise of the hateful war song (*paian*, a song of rejoicing sometimes used to celebrate victory, and thus hateful to Troy) that sounded as the Greeks approached Troy (144–7/ 126–7), and again as the cry that Hecuba will raise "like / a mother bird for her fallen chicks" (165–6/146–7), a cry that she contrasts to the songs she led in happier days to honor the gods (167–71/148–52).

148 / 128–9 *Egyptian cable* The text here is problematic but appears to carry the literal sense "the woven lesson of Egypt," a compact though circuitous phrase for rope made of papyrus, an Egyptian invention.

172–256 / 153–229 *Parodos* The choral entrance song in this play takes the form of a *kommos* (dialogue between the chorus, divided into two groups that enter successively, and Hecuba, 172–216/153–96) and a lyric ode sung and danced by the entire chorus (217–56/197–229). The entrance of the first half-chorus is motivated by Hecuba's keening; the second is called out by the first. The *kommos* continues the lyric anapests of Hecuba's monody, emphasizing the emotional connection between the women and their erstwhile queen. In subject, however, the *parodos* moves from lament for past loss to concern for what the future may hold, focusing emphatically on the women's fate and specifically on the allotment of the women to their new masters, which will give shape to the central episodes of the play.

187–90 / 168–72 These lines anticipate Cassandra's dramatic entrance and "mad scene" by showing Hecuba's special concern for her daughter, possessed by Apollo's prophetic madness as if by Dionysiac delirium. The word for her crazed state in the Greek text is *ekbakkheuousan*, "raving in Bacchic frenzy."

225–56 / 205–29 In this passage, the chorus attempt to envisage their new life in Greece. Although their first thought is of sufferings even greater than bidding farewell to all they have known and loved, the bulk of the passage is devoted to making distinctions about the places to which they hope or fear they will be sent. Thus, geographical detail soon largely supplants their immediate emotions. Comments on this passage have largely explicated the choice they make as a reflection of current Athenian opinion, especially because Athens is emphatically the women's preferred destination and Sparta the most feared. In addition, Sicily, because of the impending Athenian expedition, must have been a hot topic in Athens when the play was produced. However this may be, it is important also to observe that the lively travelogue, as it were, shows us the women's capacity to stay resilient and even hopeful in the midst of so much destruction and horror. For the various sites mentioned, see the Glossary.

232 / 209 *The land of Theseus* Athens, referred to by the name of its legendary king. The women's preference for Athens gains emphasis by their immediate rejection of Athens's great enemy, Sparta, associated of course with Helen.

249 / 223 *Renowned for the garlands it has won* The reference is apparently to the success of Sicilians, such as Hiero of Syracuse, who won victories in the Panhellenic games. Euripides uses language in these lines reminiscent of Pindar's victory odes in celebration of such triumphs.

257–597 / 230–510 *First episode* The Greek herald Talthybius, who now arrives to tell Hecuba about the disposition of the captive women, only deepens Hecuba's sufferings with the news that Cassandra is to be Agamemnon's concubine, Andromache is to be given to Neoptolemus, Achilles' son, and she herself to Odysseus. (Talthybius only alludes to Polyxena's sacrifice at the tomb of Achilles in vague terms; see note on **291**.) The bulk of the episode is taken up with the startling appearance of Cassandra, first in a state of wild, ecstatic madness, then in a calmer mood foretelling her own doom, only to reinterpret it and the city's destruction as painful victories for Troy. The second episode in turn will pick up the threads of Andromache's and Polyxena's destinies.

262–92 / 292–323 Unusually, the episode begins with a kind of *kommos*, in which Talthybius speaks to Hecuba in trimeter dialogue verse, but she answers him in a register of higher intensity, for the most part chanting in iambics and dochmiacs, a meter used to express high emotion.

275–303 / 247–77 The dramatically effective order of the revelations in this passage also reveals Hecuba's maternal concern. She has already expressed her concern for Cassandra (187–90/168–72), and here she asks after Cassandra's fate first, followed by questions about Polyxena and her daughter-in-law Andromache, before turning to her own fate.

291 / 264 *She serves Achilles' tomb* Talthybius's euphemistic shading of the terrible truth of Polyxena's sacrifice serves a double purpose: postponing Hecuba's recognition of this loss until it can be fully exploited dramatically (713–25/618–29) and giving us our first clear glimpse of the unexpected empathy of which this Greek is capable (see the Introduction, p. 24).

304–23 / 278–91 The vehemence of this attack on Odysseus may seem surprising, but both his treachery in the *Palamedes* (see the Introduction, p. 9) and the reputation for unscrupulous behavior that is a frequent element of his portrayal in Greek literature make it fully understandable. In this play, he will be responsible for the convincing the Greeks to kill Hecuba's sole surviving grandson, Astyanax (828/721).

324–5 / 292–3 The chorus leader (speaking as always for the chorus as a whole) reminds us that the ordinary women of Troy, as well as the formerly great and mighty, will share the fate of slavery and exile. A similar note will be struck again at 789–90/684–5.

326–538 / 294–461 *Cassandra scene* Just as Talthybius is sending for Cassandra, she appears, whirling burning torches in an ecstatic dance. The torches make her resemble the vengeful Fury she will indeed become (533/457), but more immediately they are part of her willful evocation of the Greek wedding ceremony, in which torches light the bridal procession to the home of the groom. As in Aeschylus's *Agamemnon*, Cassandra's first utterance is frenzied song, after which she makes, in spoken verse, the rational but paradoxical case that Troy in defeat is better off than

Greece in victory. Euripides shows us two different but not incompatible modes in which Cassandra's prophetic gifts can find expression.

341–90 / 308–340 Cassandra's monody provides a total contrast to that of Hecuba (**109–71/98–150**) in its wild dance, its highly excited, dochmiac-charged rhythms (and therefore also presumably in its music), and its content. Cassandra imagines that she is celebrating her marriage to Agamemnon in the temple of Apollo, and the language she uses is that of formal marriage, with all its religious and social connotations. In addition to the torches that light the bride's progress into marriage (**356–65/319–25**), allusions to a wedding include the repeated invocations of Hymen, god of marriage (**345/310**, etc.), and the description of the bride and bridegroom (**346–8/311–3**) and the bridal song (**385/336**) as "blessed." There is, of course, enormous irony in all of this, and Hecuba sees it simply as a sign of madness (**400–1/349–50**), but there is also a paradoxical logic to Cassandra's celebration, which becomes clear in her subsequent speech: the sham marriage of Apollo's virgin to the Greek king leads to the king's death and to her triumph in death over Troy's enemies.

343–2 / 310 *this sacred / Precinct* identified at **375/329–30** as the temple of Apollo.

363 / 323 *Hecate* A powerful goddess associated with fire and often depicted carrying torches. Hecate's more sinister aspects, including associations with sorcery and the underworld (see Glossary), are relevant here, too. For the invocation of Hecate in the context of sorcery, see Euripides' *Medea* 397 and *Ion* 1048.

367 / 326 *Euhan Euhoi* Cries used specifically in Dionysiac rites, here a sign of Cassandra's possession by a divine afflatus; cf. notes on **187–90** for the use of *ekbakkheuein*, "revel in Bacchic frenzy," to indicate her particular form of madness, and on **524–5** for her "Bacchic" adornments.

393 / 343 *O Hephaestus* As god of fire, Hephaestus is the archetypal torch-bearer.

404–469, 487–530 / 353–405, 424–461 Cassandra's two long speeches are very different in tone from her monody: rational, clearly argued, self-aware. The message, however, remains equally paradoxical: "I will stand outside my madness / Enough to show you how much luckier / Our city's lot is than the Greeks'" (**419–21/365–7**). She prophesies her own fate—to die, bringing down Agamemnon with her—with perfect lucidity, as a victory for herself worthy of a crown of triumph (**404/353**) and as revenge for her father's and brothers' deaths (**413/360**). She also explains how Troy's glory will long outlive her defeat (**446–66/386–402**).

412 / 359 *I'll kill him* This does not imply any deviation from the traditional story that Agamemnon fell at the hands of his wife Clytemnestra and her lover Aegistheus, but makes the most of Cassandra's role as an indirect cause of his death. This is explicit in her mention of *the plot . . . to butcher a mother* (**417**/363), i.e., Orestes' revenge on Clytemnestra for killing his father.

418–86 / 365–405 Cassandra's logical demonstration that the Trojans are the victors consists of showing (**446–63**/386–99) that it is they who have won glory and fame that will last forever in song and story by dying in just defense of their own country and loved ones, whereas the Greeks (**418–42**/ 365–82) killed and died far from home, for the sake of one worthless woman, exchanged what they loved for what they hated, endured separation from fatherland and family. Those who were killed even gave up proper funeral rites at home, where their wives will die widowed and their parents childless. Taken together with the prophecies of the sufferings to come for the Greeks on their way home—in Cassandra's second speech (**495–518**/431–470) as well as the gods' prologue, both of which confirm what the audience already knew to have occurred from the *Odyssey* and elsewhere—Cassandra's argument, however paradoxical, is a powerful one.

425–7 / 370–2 *slaughtered what he loved . . . for one woman's sake* A compact attack on the origins of the Greek expedition. Cassandra alludes to the bad bargain made by Agamemnon on his brother's behalf by rescuing Menelaus's worthless wife, who had left him of her own volition, at the cost of killing his own daughter Iphigenia, the sacrificial victim demanded by Artemis before his fleet could sail from Aulis. (Euripides dramatized this incident in his final play, *Iphigenia at Aulis.*)

442–5 / 383–5 Many editors regard these lines as a spurious interpolation, both on stylistic grounds and because they interrupt the main argument. They do, however, suggest a contrast to the fame the Trojans have won, and which, Cassandra implies, the Greeks do not deserve to share.

472 / 408 *made you crazy* Literally, "filled your mind with Bacchic frenzy" (*exebakkheusen phrenas*); cf. note on **187–90**.

482–3 / 420 *a perfect bedmate / For our wise leader* Literally, "a good bride for the general," which, following Talthybius's disparagement of the "crazy" Cassandra, can only be understood as an ironic comment not just on her but on Agamemnon as well.

486 / 422–3 *she's a good woman* Odysseus's wife, Penelope, was renowned through her depiction in the *Odyssey* as a women of prudence, fortitude, and fidelity.

492–3 / 428–30 *Apollo . . . told me / She'll die right here at home* This remark alludes to a story that Euripides had already employed in his *Hecuba*, where it is foretold that the queen would end her life by falling from the mast of the ship that was to have taken her to Greece, transformed into a "bitch with fiery eyes." Her tomb would be known as "Cynossema [dog's grave], a landmark for sailors" (*Hecuba*, 1269–73). None of our other sources suggest that Hecuba died at Troy, but the promontory of Cynossema was a landmark on what is now called the Gallipoli peninsula, across the Dardanelles not far from Troy. Thus, Cassandra's emphatic "right here" should probably be understood to mean not that Hecuba never left Troy, but that she only went a short way on the long voyage to Ithaca before meeting her end. Cassandra's refusal to "reproach her with the rest" (494/430) is presumably to be understood as springing from a desire to spare Hecuba the knowledge of the struggles and undignified transformation she has yet to undergo.

500–11 / 433–43 Cassandra's prophecy employs several of the best-known episodes of the *Odyssey*: Odysseus's shipwreck (book 5), the lotus-eaters, the Cyclops (9), Circe (10), the voyage to the underworld (11), Charybdis, and the Oxen of the Sun (12).

512–23 / 444–61 The final section of Cassandra's speech is delivered in trochaic tetrameter verse, a longer line that was probably the original form of spoken dialogue verse in Greek drama. Trochaic tetrameter was often used (as here) to achieve a greater solemnity.

521 / 449 *out by the grave of my beloved bridegroom* An ironic touch, because the "marriage" of Cassandra and Agamemnon continues in a kind of bitter parody of the burial of husband and wife side by side. Here, neither has received respectful burial, and it is only a heavy downpour that carries Cassandra's discarded corpse to Agamemnon's side.

524–5 / 451–2 *Farewell, you fillets of the god I loved / So well* Cassandra removes her sacred woolen headbands and tosses them to the winds. They are tokens of her dedication to Apollo, but once again the language includes an explicitly Dionysiac term, *euia*, here translated "awe." (See the notes on 367 and 187–90 for other examples.) As a proper noun, "Euios" is a cult-name of Dionysus, derived from the ritual cry *Euioi!*, similar to the *Euhan! Euhoi!* of 367/326. Cassandra's fillets are worn in honor of Apollo, but her "euia" associates them with the Bacchic ecstasy of religious possession. The gesture of flinging off the tokens of her sacred office, and some of the language, is borrowed from a more elaborate and emotional passage in Aeschylus's *Agamemnon* (1264–74), but the terrible rancor of Cassandra there, who feels that Apollo is leading her to her death, is nowhere in evidence here. In Aeschylus, Cassandra tears at her sacred tokens and hurls them to the ground. Here, she tosses them into the air, returning them to the god before she herself is defiled.

528 / 453 *Ripped from my body* The Greek word *sparagmois* ("with tearings" or "in tatters") properly refers to various kinds of mangling and rending, including the dismemberment of a sacrificial victim in Dionysiac frenzy. Using this word for the removal of her headbands thus continues the Bacchic associations of Cassandra's devotion to her god and suggests how painful the separation from him is for her.

533 / 457 *a Fury, one of three* There was no canonical number of Erinyes, as there was for the Graces or the Fates, and Cassandra is not specifying such a number; rather, she has in mind, as James Diggle has suggested, the three human agents of vengeance who will perform the role of Furies in this case: Clytemnestra, Aegistheus, and herself.

540 / 463 *your mistress sprawled on the ground* Once again, as at the outset of the play, Hecuba has fainted and lies prostrate with grief. She refuses the help of her attendants, but then rises slowly, reanimated by the desire to "sing one final time" (552/472) of her past happiness and to recount the sorrows past, present, and to come.

552-3 / 473 *so that / My old good luck intensifies your pity* Hecuba here expresses one of the guiding principles of Greek tragedy and indeed of the Western tragic tradition through most of its history: the reversal of great good fortune, the fall of the mighty, causes more pain and provokes greater pity than the troubles of those who have never known happiness and prosperity. She will return implicitly to this idea at the end of her speech with a series of half-lines that remind us of her former happiness and provide a pathetic climax to her catalog of miseries (576–80/493–497). For a different use of this idea, see 735–8/639–40 with note.

563 / 483 *butchered at the household altar* See note on 18.

590 / 505 *Yet you would help me to my feet? For what?* It appears that Hecuba has collapsed again, overwhelmed by the sorrows she has just summarized. She asks to be taken to the "straw mat" (593/507) that is now her bed, and she is presumably now accompanied to a resting place at the side of the stage, where she will remain during the choral ode that follows.

597 / 510 *Don't call him lucky until he's dead and gone* This sentiment, given its fullest expression in the dialogue between the Greek sage Solon and Croesus, king of Lydia (Herodotus *Histories* 1.30–32), appears frequently

in tragedy (for Euripides, cf. *Andromache* 100–2, *Iphigenia at Aulis* 161–3).

598–651 / 511–67 *First stasimon* Each of the three stasima (scene-dividing lyrics, sung and danced by the chorus) evokes stories and images of Troy and the Trojans. This first one retells the story of Troy's fall, beginning with the delusive joy of the moment when the Trojan horse is brought into the city, so that (as with Hecuba's just-concluded speech) a full sense of the subsequent desolation is given in the contrast. Thus, in a sense, the ode opens out and generalizes the deeply painful sense of the transience of fortune and the pain of loss given personal expression by the old queen.

598 / 511 *Sing, Muse* The stasimon opens with an epic invocation, in the dactylic meter of epic, signaling that the chorus will pursue a grand and impressive theme, but they immediately announce that it will be "in a new key / In a strange key"—not the duels and deaths of great heroes, but the destruction of a city as it was experienced by its women.

604 / 516 *the four-wheeled horse* The Greek is deliberately vague, replicating the initial impression of something strange and equivocal, the most literal sense of the words being "wagon going on four [feet]."

612–3 / 526 *our Trojan goddess, / Zeus's daughter* This refers to Athena, whose temple was on the Acropolis of Troy, referred to again at **624–5/537** as "the virgin [literally, unyoked] / Goddess of the deathless horses." The latter epithet occurs only here, and no doubt refers, as commentators suggest, to an interest in horses appropriate to a war goddess. But there is a special appropriateness here, because the Trojans are bringing the Trojan horse to her as an offering of thanksgiving—and there is a special irony for the audience, who know of Athena's support of the Greek cause (cf. 9/10 with note), to the Trojans honoring Athena with a "gleaming / Treachery" and "Troy's destruction" (**621, 623/533–5**).

657–913 / 568–798 *Second episode* Andromache is now led in on a cart with her son Astyanax and spoils of war that include Hector's great shield. The episode has three distinct sections: a *kommos* (here a lyric duet of lament, **666–700/577–607**) between Andromache and Hecuba; an iambic dialogue in which Andromache tells Hecuba of Polyxena's death (**703–810 /610–705**); and a second iambic scene, for Andromache and Talthybius, in which the herald reveals that Astyanax is to be killed and has him seized, concluded with a brief lament by Hecuba (**811–906/706–798**). The cumulative effect of the episode is devastating. Andromache consoles Hecuba regarding Polyxena's fate by calling it better than the life she herself will now be compelled to lead. Hecuba protests that life always offers hope, offering the possibility that Astyanax may yet grow up to bring Troy back to life as a reason to go on. Talthybius enters to dash that last remaining hope, and mother and son depart in different directions to their desolate fates.

657 / 568 Andromache's entrance on a cart with her son and Hector's weapons is effective on a number of levels. No royal chariot, this wagon gives a powerful visual sign of how the mighty have fallen, for like Hector's unavailing weapons, his wife and son are now mere booty to be disposed of by the conquerors. At the same time, it suggests a contrast with (and may have been suggested by) the grander entrance by chariot of the conquering general in Aeschylus's *Agamemnon*, in whose train Cassandra is also riding. There, the fall is about to take place; here, it has already happened, but there is more suffering to come.

666–700 / 577–607 The duet is notable for its high proportion of split verses, in which each interlocutor sometimes responds to the other, sometimes completes the other's phrase, sometimes pursues her own line of thought. The effect of such broken dialogues is to give dramatic form to a degree of emotion for which regular patterns of dramatic exchange seem inadequate.

667 / 578 *You cry my cry* Literally, "Why are you groaning out my *paian*?" The *paian* is properly a song of thanksgiving or triumph (see note on **139–40**), but it can be used more generally for any solemn song. Here, in conjunction with a verb of lamentation, it is used for a song of mourning.

687 / 597 *Your son* This is Paris, who escaped death when Hecuba—though she knew he was destined to be the destroyer of Troy—refused to kill him, exposing him on a hillside instead, where he was found and raised by shepherds. *Alexander*, produced with *Trojan Women*, dramatized his return to Troy and recognition as a young man (see the Introduction, p. 8).

690 / 599 *at the feet of Pallas Athena* Literally, "in front of Pallas," i.e., in Athena's temple precinct, close to her statue. The words suggest both the sacrilege of killings in a sacred place and an implied reproach to the goddess who did not protect Troy.

697 / 603 *has no city* The Greek is *erêmopolis*, which suggests both "bereft of a city" and "whose city is desolate." Several *erêmos* words elsewhere in the play describe Troy's desolation (see **15**n).

713 / 618 A *second Ajax* Agamemnon, who will force Cassandra to become his concubine. The first Ajax dragged Cassandra by force from her sanctuary in Athena's temple. See 80/70 with note.

730–88 / 634–83 Andromache's speech has often been criticized as rhetorical padding inappropriate to the character and her situation, but granting that tragic speech is far more rhetorical than what people in similarly extreme circumstances would likely say in real life, it is not difficult to see how precisely Euripides has fitted Andromache's argument to the particulars of her character and experience. We must first notice that the speech is an answer to Hecuba's point that life is always better than death, because hope inheres in life. Andromache contrasts Polyxena's death—which she regards as a lack of all suffering, the equivalent of never being born—to her own continued misery. Her virtues are those of a proper wife, an adept in every form of prudent and modest behavior (*sôphrona*) known to women ("whatever / Custom says a woman ought to do," 744–5, 645). Andromache's particular tragedy is that, having lost husband and home, her very reputation for virtue has made Neoptolemus choose her to be his concubine, thus putting her in a dilemma in which she feels she has no good choice: be a good mate to her new man and thus betray Hector, her great love, or resist Neoptolemus and earn his hatred. Her old life is gone; her new life gives her no cause for hope. This speech expresses that dilemma with force (emotional as well as rhetorical) and thereby gives as distinctive a picture of Andromache as those we have already have of Hecuba and Cassandra.

735–7 / 639–40 *But a man / Who falls from good luck into bad luck suffers / Doubly* This is a version of the sentiment expressed by Hecuba at 552–3/473, this time emphasizing the suffering of the one who undergoes the fall, not the pity such a fall arouses in others. Polyxena, now that she is dead, has no more awareness of that suffering than if she had never been born. The contrast will be with Andromache's continued life, which offers only more suffering.

750 / 652–3 *My mind was my only teacher* Andromache says she relies on her native good sense—literally, "mind from home," where "from home" (*oikothen*) has the sense of "from my own resources"—to be her teacher.

774–7 / 673–4 The sentiment and rhetorical structure of this passage are reminiscent of Andromache's famous lines from Homer's account of her meeting with Hector on the walls of Troy (*Iliad* 6, 429–30: "Hector, you are my father and my lady mother, my brother and my ardent husband"). Here, however, as part of Andromache's argument, four abstract qualities replace the affecting list of four persons, or rather roles, that Hector plays in her life.

782–8 / 679–83 Andromache concludes by reverting to her initial claims that Polyxena's death is a better fate than her life, which she considers now proved.

789–90 / 684–5 The traditional choral "tag" that separates speech from reply is used once again (cf. 324–5/292–3) to press the similarity between the fate of those who were once privileged and the ordinary women of Troy.

791–802 / 686–96 Hecuba returns to the language of ships and sailing prominent in her opening monody (see note on 114–5). Her knowledge of ships (like Hippolytus's knowledge of sex in Euripides' *Hippolytus* 1004–5) comes only secondhand, but she, like Hippolytus, is fearful of the danger and loss of control involved. Her situation is like that of the ship in a storm that must go wherever the waves carry it.

800 / 699 *Bow down to your new master* Hecuba turns to Andromache with advice drawn from her own response to the forces that have overmastered her; and yet, characteristically for this women of almost uncanny resilience, she finds hope in the very circumstances that have led Andromache to abandon it: if Hector's widow can please her new husband, then perhaps his descendants will one day return to build Troy anew.

804 / 704 *his descendants* The manuscript here reads "sons born to you," but the reference to the safety of Astyanax makes it all the more likely that descendants of Hector, not of the non-Trojan Andromache, must be meant. Two simple corrections to the text of 703–4 give the desired sense: "bring my grandson up to be the greatest help to Troy, sons born to whom" etc.

815 / 710 *don't hate me* An unexpected opening remark for a herald of the victorious Greeks, followed by further indications of Talthybius's pain and even shame at the message he is so reluctant to deliver. His discomfort is dramatically useful for the foreboding it causes Andromache and for the way it separates Talthybius from the rest of the Greeks and implicitly pronounces judgment on their actions. After haltingly revealing the truth, Talthybius steps out of his role as herald to give Andromache sympathetic counsel (833–48/726–39). As he departs with Astyanax, he explicitly shows revulsion for his own role in carrying out the child's death sentence (903–6/786–9); later, he will provide what help and comfort he can to the Trojan women (see 1359–65/1150–5 with note and the Introduction, p. 23).

817 / 711 *the common / Will of the Greeks and of Pelops's noble grandsons* The grandsons of Pelops are Agamemnon and Menelaus; the whole phrase suggests that the army as a body has ratified a decision of the two leaders.

828 / 721 *Odysseus* known for his unscrupulousness (see note on 304–23) and for his powers of persuasion; in the *Palamedes*, both were on display.

840–1 / 731–2 *We're capable of doing whatever we want with you, / Just one woman* Literally, "we are capable of doing battle with one woman." These words have seemed overly harsh to some, but they are an integral part of acknowledging the realities of the situation, which Talthybius tells Andromache she must do. If anything, the phrase "just one woman" is a sardonic reminder of the ten years' war fought for the sake of one woman, Helen.

876–8 / 764 *O Greeks, / Not even a barbarian could invent / Atrocities like this* Literally, "O Greeks, devisers of barbarian evils." A very pointed charge, coming as it does from a "barbarian" who in effect reproaches the Greeks for conduct worthy of those they claim to despise as less than civilized. (At 890/775, Andromache further emphasizes the cruelty of the Greeks by comparing them to wild animals capable of feasting on her son's flesh.) There is a similar denunciation of the barbarity of Greeks by a barbarian, King Thoas, in Euripides' *Iphigenia in Tauris* 1174. Note, however, that on the Greek stage barbarians can use "barbarian" simply to designate non-Greeks, with no implication of barbarity. Thus, Andromache speaks of "barbarians and Greeks" at 885/771, and King Theoclymenus of Egypt mentions "sailing in barbarian waters" (Euripides' *Helen* 1210).

880–8 / 766–73 Andromache turns to Helen as the ultimate cause of her suffering, preparing us for Helen's appearance in the next episode. The rhetoric here is forceful, with its elaborate apostrophe and four personifications of Helen's putative progenitors (contrast the four great qualities that Andromache praises in Hector, 770–1/674), all culminating in the one-word curse "Die!"

880–1 / 766 *daughter of Tyndareus's house, / Zeus was never your father* See note on 42.

889 / 774, 893 / 779 *hurl* The same verb (*rhiptete*) unites the fates of mother and child as they are taken on their separate paths, him to death, her to servitude.

896–8 / 780–1 Here, as often, Troy is addressed as a fellow sufferer. The chorus leader again uses the sorrows of an individual of high standing to reflect on the sufferings of all (cf. 324–5/292–3 and 789–90/684–5).

914–993 / 799–859 *Second stasimon* This song takes as its subject the story of Troy's first destruction by Greeks, during the reign of Laomedon, father of Priam, as well as of two other sons, Ganymede and Tithonus, and a daughter, Hesione. In the first pair of stanzas, the chorus recount the sacking of the city by Telamon, King of Salamis, and the mighty Heracles ("Alcmena's son," **920**/805). Heracles brought a Greek force against Troy after rescuing Hesione from a sea monster, only to be cheated of his promised reward. The second strophic pair recalls the gods' love for Ganymede and Tithonus, and it reflects on divine abandonment of the city as the betrayal of that love.

916 / 801 *the steep slope sacred to Athena* The acropolis of Athens, which can be seen from Salamis, and where, according to Athenian tradition, the goddess planted the first olive tree and won her role as the city's patron deity.

929–30 / 814–5 *the chiseled / Stonework of Apollo* Apollo, along with Poseidon, built the walls (see note on **5–6**). When Laomedon denied them their wages, Poseidon sent the sea monster from which Heracles rescued Hesione — and was denied his own reward, hence his anger at Troy.

931 / 817 *Twice in two pummeling storms* This transition returns our focus to the current destruction of Troy.

934–5 / 821–2 *Useless son / Of Laomedon* Euripides' genealogy of the Trojan kings differs from that of Homer (*Iliad* 5.265–6), who makes Ganymede a son of an earlier king, Tros. Ganymede was chosen by Zeus to be the cup-bearer of the gods on Olympus. The chorus picture him as an eternal ephebe who looks down impassively as Troy burns, her people dying in agony. He is "useless" because he can do nothing to save his erstwhile city; indeed, he no longer seems to care that his old haunts have been destroyed.

964, 967 / 840 *Love . . . Love* Erôs, a force that even Zeus cannot resist when it fires him with desire, is here not depicted as dangerous in itself (cf., e.g., Euripides' *Hippolytus* 525–44, one of many passages in Greek literature where the destructive nature of erotic passion is emphasized); rather, the chorus sadly reflect that divine passion for mortal Trojans has offered no protection for Troy, as they had believed it would (**988–91**/857).

980–1 / 852–4 *Though she herself / Married a man from here* Dawn became enamored of Tithonus and took him up to the heavens (**985–7**/855–6), where Zeus gave him immortality.

982 / 852 *her children* Memnon (who ruled over the Ethiopians and died in the fight to save Troy) and Emathion.

993 / 858 *love Troy no longer* Literally, "the love-spell for Troy is gone / dead" (see note on 48).

994–1235 / 860–1059 *Third episode* Menelaus enters to reclaim Helen, whom he plans to put to death for her transgressions. The scene plays out as though he will indeed take her back to Sparta for a public execution, although the spectators know (in the first instance from *Odyssey*, book 4, where Helen and Menelaus appear reunited as man and wife), and Euripides gives numerous hints, that she will survive. Although Helen has often been mentioned, nothing until the beginning of the episode indicates that she will appear on stage, and the episode itself is surprising in a number of ways. When Helen appears, she asks to for a chance to plead her case. Menelaus hesitates, but Hecuba persuades him to let her speak, offering to respond to her defense. Thus begins the great *agôn* (contest), a formal debate whose place in the drama has itself been much debated. Everyone would agree, however, that it effectively changes the atmosphere of suffering and lyric lament that characterizes the rest of the play for one of argument and intellectual tension. A sign of this change is the fact that the entire episode is cast in spoken iambics, with none of the lyric verse that begins and punctuates the preceding episodes, raising their emotional temperature. For an analysis of the scene, see the Introduction, pp. 19–23.

994 / 860 *How gloriously bright the sun is shining* Menelaus's jubilant entrance brings an instant and somewhat jarring change in tone. His entrance appears to be modeled on that of the Aeschylean Aegistheus at *Agamemnon* 1577, another character who arrives unexpectedly and late in the action, and who hails the light of a longed-for day that rights past wrongs. Menelaus goes on to introduce himself in something of the manner of a prologue speech, emphasizing above all the decisive end of any erotic attachment to his former wife, whose very name he will not speak (1006–7/869–70) — though indeed he names her already at 1013/877, when declaring that he has already decided to put her to death at home in Greece.

1020–5 / 884–8 Hecuba offers a prayer to Zeus in thanks for Menelaus's apparent willingness to punish the despised Helen. The prayer is remarkable, not for its rather conventional form (the listing of alternate names and qualities by which the deity may be known) but for its content. The god "who somehow cup[s] the whole earth" while nevertheless dwelling upon it is Air (or Aether), here identified with Zeus as the supreme being. Euripides employs the view of his contemporary, Diogenes of Apollonia, following Anaximenes, that Air is the primary substance on which all else depends. The "fixed law of Nature" may refer to the Heraclitean idea of a balance of opposites, "man's Mind" as in Anaxagoras's view of *nous* (mind, intelligence) as the universal animating principle. In short, Hecuba momentarily speaks in the language of philosophical and scientific speculation, a feature of this passage that has been widely criticized as a reflection of Euripides' interests rather than an expression of dramatic character. It is worth considering, however, whether the language here does not rather express the extreme experience of loss and grief that drive Hecuba to seek a new understanding of the force that can cause such things and still be imagined as guiding "the tangled / Affairs of men toward the path of Justice." And that belief (or hope) is, of course, the great irony of her strange prayer, because justice will not be done, and Hecuba's last hope will be denied.

1031 / 891 *She's hell* The pun on Helen / hell in the translation is prompted by the repeated use of a Greek verb (*haireô,* "seize," "destroy") whose aorist forms (here *helêi*) provide an etymology of the name Helen, "the destroyer," already used to wonderful effect by Aeschylus (*Agamemnon* 689–90): *helenas, helandros, heleptolis,* "destroyer of ships, of cities, of men."

1035 / 895 *Menelaus* In contrast to her husband, who initially refused even to speak her name, Helen begins by addressing him directly, and with a complaint about rough treatment, no less. Altogether, although ostensibly powerless, she is clearly an arresting and imposing figure. Her self-assurance is partly expressed on stage by her appearance. In the midst of the shorn heads and rags of the Trojan women, the still-beautiful Helen enters (as we can infer from Hecuba's censure at 1191–8/1022–8) in her full finery. Whether we are to imagine her complaints as justified — that is, whether she is (as many modern stage directions suggest) dragged in by Menelaus's soldiers, or whether she shakes them off and enters proudly, head held high — is a questions for directors and readers to decide for themselves.

1047 / 906 *Let her speak* Hecuba's motivation for permitting the debate is, perhaps, a moot point. It would tip the balance too obviously if Menelaus gave in by approving Helen's request. (Note his insistence at 1055/913 that he only grants Helen's request because Hecuba wants him to.) On the other hand, if one wishes to construct a plausible reason for Hecuba's move, at least two spring to mind. First and foremost, Hecuba understands that contact with Helen will put Menelaus's resolve at severe risk — she has advised him not even to look at her (1028–9/891, cf. 1224–6/1049–51) — and she wants to refute in advance the defense that Helen might make on another occasion without contradiction. Secondly, the debate itself makes clear that Hecuba takes a kind of grim pleasure in having this one chance to lash out formally and publicly at the person she regards as the source of all her woes.

1058–9 / 916–7 *I know exactly what / You would accuse me of* Helen's opening move
signals the fact that the ordinary order of speeches in such a debate
(in effect, a trial scene) is reversed here: defense precedes accusation. On
the other hand, Hecuba's role is precisely to refute Helen's case. In
addition, the second speech in Euripidean debates is generally the
stronger (that at *Medea* 465–975 is an exception). Ironically, despite
Menelaus's concurrence at close of scene, in the end Hecuba's arguments will not prevail with him.

1061–85 / 919–37 The first part of Helen's defense is a series of attacks against those she
says should be held responsible, rather than herself, for everything that has
happened. She begins with Paris, destined from birth to destroy his city,
and along with him Priam and Hecuba, who knew of his destiny but let
him live. Next, she indicts Aphrodite, who offered Helen as Paris's prize
should she win the beauty contest with the other goddesses on Mount Ida.
Pointing out that the prizes offered by her competitors involved Greece's
domination by Troy, Helen concludes that, because she was chosen and
thus kept Greece from enslavement to a tyrant, she should receive a crown
of honor from the Greeks, rather than their hatred.

1066–7 / 922 *Alexander, as he was called then, / The murderous firebrand Hecuba
dreamed of* Both Alexander's renaming as Paris and Hecuba's dream
while pregnant with him that she was giving birth to a firebrand were
recounted in *Alexander*, the first of the plays performed with *Trojan
Women* (see the Introduction, p. 8).

1086–1117 / 938–65 Helen defends her own actions, emphasizing the irresistible power
of Aphrodite and placing the blame on the goddess for her elopement
with Paris. She then excuses herself for not returning to Menelaus after
Paris's death by claiming that she tried to do so but was thwarted, an
assertion that cannot any longer be put to the test (see note on 1109–10).

1105 / 952 *Once Paris was dead and buried* Paris was killed by Philoctetes, using one of
Heracles' poisoned arrows.

1109–10 / 956 *The tower guards will tell you…And the watchmen from the walls* A
convenient claim, because the men of Troy have all been killed and
cannot testify to anything.

1113–7 / 961–5 A formal summation, as befits the judicial character of the debate,
addressed to Menelaus as judge.

1121–62 / 969–1001 Answering Helen, Hecuba's speech also falls into two main divi-
sions. In the first, she caustically deconstructs Helen's argument for the

responsibility of the gods, concluding that "Aphrodite" here is merely another name for Helen's own lust and that she went to Troy willingly. As part of her case for Helen's responsibility, Hecuba denies the mythical tradition of the Judgment of Paris ("a silly Miss Olympus / Competition," 1129–30/975). (For more on this rationalist line of argument, see the Introduction, pp. 21–2.)

1143–4 / 986 *and all / Of Amyclae as well* This city, in close proximity to Sparta, was associated through legend and monuments with the Heroic Age (see Pausanias *Description of Greece* 3.18.7–19.6).

1148 / 989 *lust run wild* Literally, "foolish things," but the word in question (*môros*) can refer, especially in Euripides, to sexual intemperance specifically.

1149–50 / 990 *"witless" rhymes / With Cypris* Literally, "the goddess's name rightly begins with [the word for] folly," a pun on the name *Aphro-dite*, "the foam-born one," and *a-phrosyne*, "lack of sense."

1162 / 1001 *Not yet ascended to the stars* Euripides alludes to the legend that, after their death, Helen's brothers were deified. He is the first surviving author to connect them with stars; they are later commonly identified with the constellation Gemini (the Twins). As deities, they were invoked for rescue, especially at sea. Hecuba's point here is that while they were still alive, they could easily have rescued their sister, had she only called out to them.

1163–1203 / 1002–31 The second part of Hecuba's speech deals with Helen's actions in Troy and refutes her attempts to exculpate herself. Hecuba concludes with two powerful apostrophes, telling Helen that she should be ashamed to appear in all her finery amidst the misery she has caused, and telling Menelaus that his honor, and that of husbands everywhere, depends on his killing of Helen.

1200–1 / 1030–1 *crown your country's honor with a deed / Worthy of your own* Hecuba's summation replaces Helen's conceit of receiving a crown of honor from Greece (1085/937) with the image of her death as a crown of honor for Greece, and for Menelaus.

1217 / 1042 *I'm on my knees* Literally, "[I beg you] by your knees," a characteristic gesture of supplication. Helen uses a powerful weapon here, and Hecuba quickly intervenes to defuse it.

1224–6 / 1049–51 Menelaus replies to Hecuba's sensible suggestion that he not risk taking Helen back on his own ship with what can only be a joke, or at least an attempt at one—something obviously very rare in classical tragedy. It may be that he is derisively shrugging off the implication of his own weakness, or it may be simply a sign of his insensitivity to the tragic implications of the situation. In any case, Hecuba ignores his remark and makes her point clear. To the audience, her final warning is poignant, because they know that Menelaus will indeed succumb to temptation.

1236–1319 / 1060–1117 *Third stasimon* This ode continues the theme of the gods' abandonment of Troy broached in the preceding stasimon. There, however, the subject was treated somewhat obliquely, evoking the unconcern for the present sufferings of Troy on the part of the divine lovers of Trojans from earlier days—Zeus, who made Ganymede his favorite and the cup-bearer of the gods (**934–63**/820–39), and Dawn, who married Tithonus (**964–93**/840–59). Here, the Trojan women permit themselves to reproach Zeus directly and with unconcealed bitterness. The first strophic pair frames a long, highly evocative description of Troy's beautiful setting and the rites celebrated to honor its gods with direct addresses to the god, rebuking him for his betrayal and expressing dismay at his callous lack of concern for Troy's destruction. The second strophe strikes a surprisingly intimate note: the women first address their husbands, whom they picture unburied and wandering as restless shades, then lament their own departure into slavery. Finally, they evoke the cries of their children, afraid of being separated from their mothers as they, too, are sent to the ships to be taken far away. In the second antistrophe, the chorus return to Zeus, hoping despite everything to enlist his aid—not for themselves but for the destruction of Helen and Menelaus before they reach home in Sparta. Their scorn for Helen comes as no surprise following her "trial," but the fact that Menelaus is depicted as having "got back" his wife (**1315**/1114), with no mention of his promise to see to her execution in Sparta, suggests that the women understand that Helen will survive Troy's ruin, and their own, unscathed.

1242 / 1065 *sacred Pergamum* The epithet underlines the irony of a city that has honored its gods and been hallowed by them but has now been destroyed with their consent. The point is reinforced at **1249**/1070 by the characterization of the entire Trojan territory as "luminous and holy."

1250 / 1071 *Gone Phroudos* (see note on **48**) is given emphasis by its position in the phrase; the list of religious celebrations, rites, and objects that follows serves both to evoke nostalgically what has been lost and to reproach the gods who have turned away from all these honors and devotions.

1256–7 / 1075–6 *sacrificial / Moon cakes, twelve in all* Literally "holy moons, twelve in number." The precise meaning is uncertain, and some editors have suggested a reference to a rite performed on the first day of the lunar month. More likely, however, is a mention of the moon-shaped sacrificial cake known to us from a surviving fragment of Euripides' *Erechtheus* (frag. 350 Kannicht).

1265–7 / 1082–3 *unburied . . . you'll wander* The widespread belief that the souls of the unburied could not find rest in the underworld and wandered about restlessly is attested for the Greeks from Homer (*Iliad* 23.71–4) onward.

1272–3 / 1087–8 *walls / Cyclopes built* Impressed by the enormous stones that made up the walls of Mycenaean citadels such as Mycenae itself, later Greeks ascribed them to the giant Cyclopes, said by Hesiod (*Theogony* 139–46) to have been mighty craftsmen.

1288–90 / 1097–8 *high peak / Of the Isthmus / Between two seas* Acrocorinth, the highest point on the northeastern corner of the Peloponnese, looks out over the gulfs on both sides of the Isthmus of Corinth.

1291 / 1099 *Where Pelops set his palace gates* Literally, "where the seat of Pelops has its gates." Peloponnese means "island of Pelops," and the "high peak" at its connection to the main land mass of Greece is metaphorically the gateway to his land.

1305–6 / 1107–8 *In her hand the golden / Mirror* Helen's mirror is a symbol of her beauty, but also of her continued life of luxury and interest in appearance. The fact that it is made of gold is significant. Once an attribute of wealthy Troy (cf. the golden statues of the gods at **1255–6/1074** and the earlier image of Paris's seductive appearance in Sparta, "his gold all glittering," at **1151/992**), now it makes a striking contrast with the misery of the Trojan captives in their rags. Beyond that, the allure of gold that attaches to both Helen and Paris is marked as something deceptive and dangerous, like the "fine harness of gold" (**520/607**) that added to the Trojan horse's glamour.

1314 / 1113 *The bronze gate of Athena's temple* Literally, "the brazen-gated goddess," a reference to a famous bronze-plated temple of Athena that stood on Sparta's acropolis.

1315–6 / 1114–5 *he's got back / The shame of Greece* Editors disagree about whether to read *echôn* ("having/holding," the manuscript reading) or *helôn* ("having taken/seized," Wilamowitz's emendation). The latter has the advantage of alluding to Helen's name through its supposed etymology from *hel-* ("seize, destroy," see note on 1031).

1320–1593 / 1118–1332 *Exodos* The concluding scene of the play is built around a ritual that is also a moment of deeply affecting intimacy: the funeral rite for Astyanax, and indeed for Troy, performed by his grandmother and the other Trojan women. That completed, the women begin their departure to a new life as slaves in Greece.

1332–3 / 1126–8 These lines allude to a story about Peleus (Neoptolemus's grandfather). Peleus accidentally killed Eurytion during the Calydonian boar hunt and went to Iolcus to be purified by King Acastus and take part in the funeral games for Pelias. That Acastus drove Peleus from Iolcus appears to be a Euripidean variant; the real significance of the allusion, however, appears to be what Euripides left unsaid but most in his audience would already know: that Peleus, fleeing Iolcus, went to meet Neoptolemus on his way home from Troy but was shipwrecked and died on the island of Cos—a further prediction of Greek suffering to come.

1359–65 / 1150–5 Talthybius's touching account of Andromache's plea for her child's burial ends with a surprising announcement that he has already washed the body (ordinarily performed by female relatives) and that he will now go dig the grave. His expressed interest in speeding the departure does not negate the impression he conveys of deep sympathy for the Trojan women's suffering.

1366–1422 / 1156–99 Hecuba's lament over the body of Astyanax is in effect a formal funeral oration, presented as a series of apostrophes: to the Greeks, in outrage at their killing of an innocent child; to the boy whose life has so brutally been cut short, with a series of tenderly intimate reminiscences; and to the shield of Hector, the reminder of a father's lost greatness that now will serve as the child's tomb. Euripides has chosen to forgo a more conventional messenger speech describing Astyanax's death in favor of giving the pathos of his loss, and even the damage to his body, a far more personal and touching expression in the words of his loving grandmother.

1393 / 1176 *Like wicked laughter between the bones* Literally "laughs out from the broken bones," a deliberately grotesque metaphor. Hecuba, as she goes on to say, will not cover over the shameful ugliness of the violence done.

1426–30 / 1203–6 The very sententiousness of Hecuba's conclusion reminds us that sudden reversal of fortune does not afflict the Trojans only. As Poseidon and Athena prophesied, and Cassandra reminded us, the Greeks will suffer destruction in turn.

1443–83 / 1216–50 The first of two *kommoi* (lyric exchanges) that end the play. This one brings the funeral rites for Astyanax to a close, Hecuba replying to the chorus's lyric keening largely in spoken iambics as she adorns the corpse of her grandson with the such gifts as the Trojan women still have to bestow.

1445–6 / 1216–7 *you / Who were once a great prince in my city* Refers to Astyanax, despite the fact (and perhaps emphasizing it) that he did not live to rule. The Greek words translated "great prince in my city" (*anaktôr poleôs*, "ruler of the city") is a version of the boy's name, *Asty-* ("city") *anax* ("ruler").

1456 / 1225 *that cunning liar* Odysseus persuaded the Greeks to kill Astyanax (828/721, and see note on **304–23**).

1472–78 / 1240–45 Hecuba despairs of the gods who have abandoned her city (a theme introduced by Poseidon himself **28/25** and broached by the Chorus in their second and third odes), and yet even now she attempts to find some good in Troy's catastrophe. Had the gods not brought Troy down, her people would never have won fame in song and story, the only guarantee of survival after death. Cassandra had made the same claim to validate the glory of Hector and Paris (**454–62/394–99**). As ironic as this might sound to us, it will have resonated with ancient Greeks, reinforced not only by the beloved poems of Homer but by tragedies like this one.

1484–98 / 1251–9 A short choral outburst in sung anapests brings the rites for Astyanax to an end as his body is carried out, then calls our attention to the walls of Troy, where men are said to have appeared carrying lighted torches. These are the "captains" (**1499/1260**) whom Talthybius orders to set the city ablaze. It is not necessary to suppose that such men appeared on the roof of the stage building; we are simply asked to imagine their presence. Indeed, the invitation to look may have a double function, because this is the point in many Euripidean tragedies when a god appears above the stage, but no god will come to the rescue here.

1524–5 / 1282–3 *Better to die / Here* Hecuba has reached the breaking point at last. Seeing her city burn as she is ordered to the Greek ships, she rushes to die in the "pyre" that was her city. "Better to die" recalls Hecuba's refutation of Andromache's similar sentiment (**726–9/630–3**).

1529–93 / 1287–1332 The final *kommos* is a kind of funeral lament for Troy. Hecuba, stopped from self-destruction, frees herself from her captors and begins the dirge with a piercing cry. The *kommos* is a good example of how classical drama can express powerful emotion in formally rigorous structures: two strophic pairs made up of lyric iambics with a very high number of resolutions (long syllables divided into two shorts) adding to an overwhelming sense of emotional urgency and force. This force is underlined by Hecuba's powerful gesture of beating the earth with her hands (**1553**/1306), taken up by the Chorus, who explain it as a means of calling forth the spirits of the dead (**1555–7**/1308–9).

1538–44 / 1295–1301 The text of this antistrophe is very uncertain. We have followed Diggle's edition in omitting two lines at the end of the antistrophe (1300–1) that refer to the burning of Troy and are likely to have been connected in some way to the textually corrupt **1538–41**/1295–7. Alan Shapiro translates the omitted lines:

> While fire and the hungry blades
> Go rioting
> From room to room.

1589 / 1328 As the towers shake and the city falls to ruins, Hecuba rises one last time and leads the women away to their new lives. On the significance of this gesture, see the Introduction, p. 25.

GLOSSARY

ACASTUS: King of Iolcus, son of Pelias; at his father's funeral games, he
purified Peleus from the accidental killing of a companion at
the Calydonian boar hunt; in *Trojan Women* **1333**/1127–8, he is
said to have subsequently exiled Peleus from Iolcus.

ACHAEAN, ACHAEANS: Synonym for "Greek," "Greeks" in Homer and
later literature. In historical times, Achaea was the name of a
region in the northern Peloponnese.

ACHILLES: Greatest of the Greek warriors at Troy, son of Peleus and the
goddess Thetis, father of Neoptolemus; his killing by Hector is
the culminating event of the *Iliad*. He is killed by an arrow from
Paris's bow, and Polyxena is sacrificed at his tomb as an offering
to his shade.

AEGEAN: Sea that divides Greece from Asia Minor.

AGAMEMNON: King of Mycenae, supreme leader of the Greek forces at
Troy, murdered upon his return home by his wife Clytemnestra
and his cousin Aegistheus, her lover.

AJAX: Son of Oileus, from Locri, sometimes referred to as the "lesser
Ajax," to distinguish him from Ajax, son of Telamon and leader
of the troops from Salamis at Troy. This Ajax, though depicted
in the *Iliad* as a valiant fighter, is best known for a sacrilege that
caused the death of much of the Greek army on its voyage back
from Troy. Ajax seized Cassandra by force from the statue of
Athena, to which she clung as a suppliant after the fall of her
city. In retribution, Athena sent a terrible storm that wrecked a
large number of Greek ships, including the one on which Ajax
was sailing.

ALCMENA: Wife of Amphytrion, King of Thebes, and beloved of Zeus, to whom she bore Heracles, the greatest of Greek heroes.

ALEXANDER: An alternate name for Paris.

AMYCLAE: A city celebrated for its connections to heroes of the Heroic Age, situated on the banks of the Eurotas just south of Sparta.

ANDROMACHE: Wife of Hector, the greatest of the Trojan warriors, daughter-in-law of Hecuba, mother of Astyanax; allotted as a war prize to Neoptolemus, son of Achilles (who killed her husband), to be his concubine.

APOLLO: Prophetic god of Delphi, leader of the Muses, god of healing and purification, among other powers. The son of Zeus and Leto, he also appears under the names Phoebus ("bright one") and Loxias ("crooked one," explained as referring either to the oblique orbit of the sun, with which he is often identified, or to the obscurity of his oracles).

ARCADIANS: Inhabitants of Arcadia, a mountainous region of the central Peloponnese.

ARGIVE: Inhabitant or attribute of Argos.

ARGOS: Major city of the Argive plain in the Peloponnese, often conflated with Mycenae as the royal seat of Agamemnon.

ARTEMIS: Sister of Apollo, virgin goddess who presides over childbirth and is pictured both as hunter and protector of wild animals.

ASTYANAX: Son of Hector and Andromache, who does not live to fulfill the meaning of his name, "ruler of the city."

ATHENA: Virgin goddess born full grown and armed from the head of Zeus, associated with arts and handicrafts, especially weaving, but also a warrior goddess. She sided with the Greeks at Troy but turned against them because of their sacrilegious behavior in victory.

ATHENS: Chief city of Attica, where Greek tragedy was performed at the festivals of Dionysus.

ATREUS: Son of Pelops, father of Agamemnon and Menelaus, he murdered his brother's children and served them to their father
Thyestes at a horrendous feast, giving his name to a house torn
apart by deceit, murder, and revenge.

CAPHEREUS: A promontory on the southeastern coast of Euboea, where
the rocky coast was dangerous for ships.

CARTHAGE: Phoenician city on the African coast.

CASSANDRA: Daughter of Priam and Hecuba allotted to Agamemnon after the fall of Troy. Apollo gave her the gift of
prophecy, but when she refused his sexual advances, he
punished her with the curse that her prophecies would
never be believed.

CASTOR and POLLUX: Twin sons of Zeus and Leda, known collectively
as the Dioscuri. After their deaths, they were taken to the
heavens as gods and became known for rescuing those in
danger, especially mariners at sea.

CHARYBDIS: A sea monster whose swallowing and disgorging of great
quantities of water, producing the effect of a whirlpool, made it
dangerous to sail near her. Odysseus, when first passing between her and Scylla, another monstrous creature, escapes
unharmed; returning, he is caught up in the whirlpool and
only saves himself by clinging to a fig tree at the mouth of
Charybdis's cave.

CRATHIS: River in the instep of Italy's boot that flows into the Ionian
Sea near the eighth-century Greek colony of Sybaris, which
became a byword for luxury. Athens had a direct connection to
this area: Sybaris was destroyed in 510 and refounded as Thurii
by Athenians in 443.

CRONUS: Youngest son of Heaven and Earth, who overcame his father
to become leader of the Titans. He in turn was defeated and
supplanted as chief of the gods by Zeus,. youngest of his six
children by his sister Rhea.

CYCLOPES: Gigantic one-eyed beings. In the *Odyssey*, they appear to
belong to a pastoral but savage race; in Hesiod's *Theogony*, they
are splendid craftsmen who make Zeus's thunderbolts. In line
with this second tradition, they are credited with building the

"Cyclopean" walls of cities like Mycenae, built from huge, beautifully fitted boulders.

CYPRIS: "The Cyprian goddess," a cult name of Aphrodite taken from her shrine on Cyprus.

DARDANIAN: Another name for the Trojan, derived from Dardanus.

DARDANUS: Founder of Troy and ancestor of Priam.

EPEIUS: A Greek from Phocis who devised the Trojan Horse as the means to end the war at last.

ETNA: Volcano still active in Sicily, "the land of Etna." Etna is the "stronghold of Hephaestus" because of the tradition that its eruptions were caused by the god's work in his forge under the mountain.

EUBOEA: The island that stretches alongside the Greek mainland from Attica to Thessaly.

EUROTAS: River of Sparta; used metonymically to refer to Sparta.

HECATE: Goddess of the underworld, crossroads, and magic; also (like Artemis) worshipped as a nurturer of children and thus connected to marriage.

HECTOR: Son of Priam and Hecuba, husband of Andromache, father of Astyanax. The greatest of the Trojan warriors, he was killed by Achilles, the greatest warrior of the Greeks.

HECUBA: Queen of Troy, wife of Priam and mother of, among others, Hector, Paris, Polyxena, and Cassandra.

HELEN: Daughter of Leda and Zeus (or Tyndareus), wife of Menelaus. Her legendary beauty led to her abduction (or seduction) by Paris, which led in turn to the Trojan War.

HEPHAESTUS: Son of Zeus and Hera, god of fire and the forge.

HERA: Goddess of marriage, wife and sister of Zeus, she sides against Troy when Paris awards Aphrodite the prize for being the most beautiful. Hera is called the Argive goddess because of her famous sanctuary and cult at Argos.

HERACLES: Son of Zeus and Alcmena, a mighty fighter of the generation before the Trojan War whose preferred weapon was the bow. He destroyed the earlier walls of Troy after he had been denied the horses promised as a reward for rescuing Hesione, daughter of King Laomedon, from a monster. After his death, this godliest of heroes, in both accomplishments and appetites, became a god.

HYMENAEUS (or simply HYMEN):   A god, or in some explanations a particularly handsome man who married happily, invoked for good fortune in chants accompanying the bridal procession.

IDA: A mountain near Troy, site of the Judgment of Paris.

ILIUM: An alternate name for Troy.

IONIAN SEA: The sea that lies between the Balkan peninsula and Italy, today usually called the Adriatic.

ISTHMUS: The Isthmus of Corinth, the neck of land connecting the Peloponnese to the rest of mainland Greece.

LAERTES: Father of Odysseus.

LAOMEDON: King of Troy and, in Euripides' genealogy, father of Ganymede, Tithonus, and Priam.

LEMNOS: Island in the northeast Aegean.

LIGURIAN: Inhabitant of Liguria, an area on the northwest coast of Italy.

LOXIAS: See APOLLO.

MENELAUS: King of Sparta, brother of Agamemnon, and husband of Helen.

MYKONOS: Island in the Aegean Sea.

NEOPTOLEMUS: Son of Achilles, who fought at Troy after his father's death and killed Priam during the sack of Troy; awarded Andromache as a war prize.

NEREIDS: The fifty daughters of the sea god Nereus, who live in the depths of the Aegean.

ODYSSEUS: King of Ithaca, son of Laertes; known for cunning wiles and persuasive speech.

OLYMPUS: Mountain in northeastern Thessaly; home of the Olympian gods.

PALLAS: Alternate name or title of Athena.

PARIS: Son of Priam and Hecuba, also known as Alexander. Exposed at birth because of a prophecy that he would destroy Troy, he was rescued by a shepherd. He returned to Troy as a young man and was recognized. Paris's abduction of Helen while a guest of Menelaus in Sparta brought about the Trojan War and the eventual death of his city.

PARNASSUS: Mountain of Phocis in central Greece.

PEIRENE: Fountain at Corinth, famous for the clarity of its waters.

PELEUS: King of Phthia in Thesssaly, mortal husband of the Nereid Thetis, who bore their son Achilles, and grandfather of Neoptolemus.

PELIAS: King of Iolcus in Thessaly.

PELOPS: King of Argos who gave his name to the Peloponnese ("island of Pelops"); grandfather of Agamemnon and Menelaus.

PENEUS: River in Thessaly that flows to the sea between Olympus and Ossa.

PHTHIA: Region of Thessaly over which Peleus and his descendants ruled.

PERGAMUM: Alternate name for Troy, from a word meaning "citadel."

PHOCIS: A region of central Greece around Mount Parnassus.

PHOEBUS: See APOLLO.

PHRYGIA, PHRYGIANS: Alternate names for Troy, Trojans.

PITANE: A district in the city of Sparta.

POLLUX: See Castor.

POLYXENA: Unmarried daughter of Priam and Hecuba, sacrificed at Achilles' tomb to appease his shade.

PRIAM: King of Troy, son of Laomedon and husband of Hecuba; father of many children, including Hector, Paris, Cassandra, and Polyxena.

SALAMIS: Island near Athens; Telamon's realm.

SCAMANDER: River at Troy.

SIMOIS: River at Troy.

SKYROS: Island in the Aegean Sea.

SPARTA: Principal city of the southern Peloponnese, ruled by Menelaus; original home of Helen of Troy. In the fifth century, Athens's chief enemy in the Peloponnesian War.

TALTHYBIUS: Herald of the Greek army.

TELAMON: King of Salamis who with Heracles destroyed the walls of Troy a generation before the Trojan War. Father of Ajax, the greatest Greek warrior at Troy after Achilles.

THEBES: Chief city of Boeotia; in the fifth century, an important opponent of Athens in the Peloponnesian War.

THESEUS: King of Athens in the generation prior to the Trojan War.

THESSALY: A large region in northern Greece.

TROY: City in northwestern Asia Minor near the Hellespont (today, Dardanelles), site of the Trojan War. Its inhabitants are barbarians (non-Greeks), although they are regularly depicted as being practically indistinguishable from Greeks in language, customs, and religion.

TYNDAREUS: King of Sparta, husband of Leda; the "mortal father" of Helen and other children said to have been sired by Zeus.

ZEUS: Chief and most powerful of the gods, father of many deities and mortals, including Apollo, Athena, Heracles, and Helen.

FOR FURTHER READING

Barlow, Shirley A., ed. and trans., *Euripides: Trojan Women* (Warminster, 1986). (This is a useful edition, using Diggle's standard text and providing a quite literal translation along with a thoughtful introduction and notes.)

Burnett, Anne P. "*Trojan Women* and the Ganymede Ode." *Yale Classical Studies* 25 (1977): 291–316.

Croally, N. T. *Euripidean Polemic:* The Trojan Women *and the Function of Tragedy* (Cambridge, 1994).

Gilmartin, Kristine. "Talthybius in *The Trojan Women*." *American Journal of Philology* 91 (1970): 213–22.

Havelock, Eric. "Watching the Trojan Women." In *Euripides: A Collection of Critical Essays*, ed. E. Segal, 115–27. Englewood Cliffs, N.J., 1968.

Poole, Adrian. "Total Disaster: Euripides' *The Trojan Women*." *Arion* New Series 3 (1976): 257–87.

CPSIA information can be obtained
at www.ICGtesting.com
Printed in the USA
BVHW050250100723
666980BV00006B/19

9 780195 179101